HYPNOTISM AND MYSTICISM OF INDIA

Preface

This book is the first of its kind that presents the secrets of Oriental Hypnotism (Maya) and the Real Magic of India. Its author, Ormond McGill, is a hypnotist of international reputation, and has toured as "The Dean of American Hypnotists" to many parts of the world presenting his famous "Concert of Hypnotism" Programs.

The original draft of this work was written in Calcutta in collaboration with Sahdu Parimal Bandhu, who is a Hindu sage of great knowledge. Most likely it was because of his warm friendship and his appreciation of Ormond McGill's professional interst in hypnotism and the real magic of India that he so generously revealed these secrets of Hypnotic (Maya) and Yoga Mystical Teachings. Also, the Sadhu was a man of high intuitive powers, so it is entirely possible that he sensed the time was right for now opening to western hypnotists this phase of the esoteric wisdom of India.

Following an introduction in which Ormond McGill tells of the importance and exclusive nature of the material in this book, he explains how some of the world renowned feats of Hindu Fakir Magic are performed. Next, he gives you in depth instructions for performing the real Magic of the Mind, exactly as the advanced Hindu magicians are taught. You are shown how to control prana through Pranayama, Oriental Breathing Techniques, The Power of Yoga Concentration, Visualization and Projection of Thought, The Magic Force of Words and Sounds, Silent Psychic Influencing, and Yogi Mental Broadcasting. You proceed on into a knowledge of the High Magic of India, and are taught the reading of the Akashic Records, Astral Projection, and Yoga Cosmology. And you learn how to perform Yama, the Yoga Method of Self-Development. Of tremendous interest to hypnotists throughout the world, Ormond McGill teaches you the Yogi Art of Maya, and gives you his exclusive Occidental/Oriental Techniques of Hypnotizing.

Among the previously published books of Ormond McGill are his outstanding *Professional Stage Hypnotism,* which we published. It is with real pride that I am now able to bring to the hypnotic fraternity this valuable work, *The Hypnotism and Mysticism of India.*

Gil Boyne, President
Westwood Publishing Company

HYPNOTISM AND MYSTICISM OF INDIA

Ormond McGill

WESTWOOD PUBLISHING CO.
700 S. Central Ave.
Glendale, CA 91204
(818) 242-1159

Library of Congress Cataloging in Publication Data

McGill, Ormond.
    Former title: The Mysticism and magic of India.

    Includes index.
    1. Hypnotism 1. Magic — India I. Title
ISBN 0-930298-01-2

PRINTED IN THE UNITED STATES OF AMERICA

Contents

Charminar, the pride of Hyderabad. It was built as a talisman by Sultan Mohammed Quili Qutab Shan to drive away pestilence from his land, and today stands as an impressive monument of India's ancient culture amidst the bustle of city life.

Acknowledgments

This book teaches of Yoga, but it deals with a phase of Yoga about which you may never have heard. It also opens new avenues of thought as it presents new laws, principles, and universal concepts that are Oriental in nature. Some may find what they will read startling as this knowledge is not given as abstract theories but is presented for actual performance; for these are "the hidden teachings" which provide instructions of the practice of magic for the magicians of India.

The original draft of this work was written in Calcutta, India in collaboration with Sadhu Parimal Bandhu. Those who are familiar with my book, "The Secret World of Witchcraft," and the book, "Religious Mysteries of the Orient," coauthored with my partner, Ron Ormond, will recognize the name of Parimal Bandu. Parimal Bandu is a Hindu Sage of magnificent knowledge. I am certain that it was because of his warm friendship for Ron and his appreciation of my professional interest in magic, as an American magician and hypnotist, that he so generously revealed these secrets of Yoga magical teachings. Also, the Sadhu was a man of high intuitive powers, so it is entirely possible that he sensed the time as being right for opening to western people this phase of the esoteric wisdom of the Orient.

I am dedicating this book to two fine men, my partner, Ron Ormond, without whose spirit of adventure this knowledge could never have been sought, and the great Avatar, Sadhu Parimal Bandhu who made possible this writing of the real magic of India.

Also, I wish to express appreciation to the following people and sources who have made possible the picture gallery of India and magic which has been used to illustrate this book: the American Consulate General, Calcutta, India; Ron Ormond (with permission of A. S. Barnes & Company, Inc.); world traveler magician and hypnotist, Arnold Furst; Benjamin J. Kleinman, International Ambassador for The Society of American Magicians; P. C. Sorcar, Official Ambassador of Magic for the Government of India; Yog Kohi and Bina Murti, Directors, Government of India Tourist Offices; Rabindra Seth, Public Relations Manager, India Tourism Development Corporation of New Delhi, the Oxford Book & Stationery Company of Calcutta, Moonyeen De Silva of Sri Lanka, Prof. S. C. Bose, the Bose Collection of India; renowned magician and magic historian, Milbourne Christopher, and the Great Virgil from his extensive tours in India.

This ancient carving at Mahabalipuram is known as "The Penance of Arjuna." The face of a huge whale-shaped rock has been carved into a massive base relief believed to be the largest in the world. It depicts Lord Arjuna in the act of doing penance so as to obtain a boon from Lord Shiva. Besides the animals, gods, and angels, the mythical story of the river Ganga issuing from its source in the Himalayas and fables from the Panchatantra have been sculptured with remarkable realism.

Introduction

This book is the third of a series; 1 *The Secret World Of Witchcraft*, 2 *Religious Mysteries Of The Orient*, and 3 *The Mysticism And Magic Of India* completes the trilogy.

"East is east and west is west, and never the twain shall meet." This book breaks that classic, and brings to western people the secret knowledge of the East. Thus, while the main purpose is to teach you the performance of India's wonderful magic, it provides additional rewards in giving you instructions which will enrich your life in many ways.

India is popularly known as "The Land of Magic." Tourists who visit that fabled land are fascinated with the remarkable feats of magic they see the fakirs perform in the market places, and return with tales of wonders. Scholars who have probed into oriental lore have discovered far deeper knowledge which is *the real magic of India*.

There are in reality two Indias, one "the surface India," which is the India the tourist finds fascinating in discovering an exotic new world of glitter and enchantment with ways of life unique to the west; and then there is "the hidden India" which was born of long past yesteryears when she was the "mother country" of magical knowledge. This is the India which is the storehouse of the ancient wisdom; this is the India which the average tourist never sees.

The Orient has always been looked upon as the great fount of inner knowledge and as the original home of the mysteries. Orders of Antiquity make reference to this realization in their ceremonies, "Look to the East, for from the East cometh light." This speaks of that ancient wisdom, and, for the seeker, in India can still be found the secrets of the ages, for the ancient wisdom continues to be treasured and the secret doctrines are taught—*but by the few and to the few*. This book probes those secrets.

Here is what leading authorities have to say as to the importance of these teachings:

Victor Cousin, the celebrated French writer, says, "When we read the poetical and philosophical monuments of the East, above all those of India, which are beginning to spread to western countries, we discover there many a truth, and truths so profound, and which make such a contrast with the meanness of the results at which occidental genius has sometimes stopped, that we are constrained to bend the knee before the philosophy of the East, and to see in this cradle of the human race the native land of the highest knowledge. India contains the whole history of philosophy in a nutshell."

Sir Monier Williams, of scientific fame, says, "If I may be allowed the anachronism, the Hindus were Spinozites more than two thousand years before the existence of Spinoza; and Darwinians many centuries before Darwin; and evolutionists many centuries before the doctrines of evolution had been accepted by the scientists of our time; indeed, before the word 'evolution' existed in any language in the world."

Professor E. W. Hopkins, writes, "Plato was full of Sankhyan thought, worked out by him, but taken from Pythagoras. Before the sixth century B.C. all the religious-philosophical ideas of Pythagoras were current in India. If there were but one or two of these cases, they might be set aside as accidental coincidences, but such coincidences are too numerous to be the result of chance. Neo-Platonism and Christian Gnosticism owe much to India. The Gnostic ideas go back directly to Hindu sources. Soul and Light were one in the Sankyha system, before they became so in Greece; and when they appeared united in Greece, it was by means of the thought that was borrowed from India. The famous Three Gunas of the Sankyha reappeared as the Gnostic 'Three Classes.' "

Davies says, "Kapila's System is the first formulated system of philosophy of which the world has a record. It is the earliest attempt on record to give an answer, from reason alone, to the mysterious questions which arise in every thoughtful mind about the origin of the world, the nature and relations of man, and his future destiny. The philosophy of Schopenhauer and Hartmann is a reproduction of the philosophical system of Kapila in its materialistic part, presented in a more elaborate form, but on the same fundamental lines. In this respect, the human mind has gone over the same ground that it occupied more than two thousand years ago; but on a more important question it has taken a step in retreat. Kapila recognized fully the existence of a soul in man, forming, indeed, his proper nature—the absolute of Fischte—distinct from matter and immortal; but our latest philosophy, here and in Germany, can see in man only a highly developed organization."

Hopkins says, "Both Thales and Parmenides were indeed anticipated by the Hindu sages, and the Eleatic School seems but a reflection of the Upanishads. The doctrines of Anaxamander and Heraclitus *were not known first* in ancient Greece."

Schlegel says, "The divine origin of man, as taught in the Vedanta, is continually inculcated to stimulate his efforts to return, to animate him in the struggle, and to incite him to consider a reunion and reincorporation with his Source as the one primary object of every action and reaction. Even the loftiest philosophy of the Europeans, the idealism of reason as it is set forth by the Greek philosophers, appears in comparison with the abundant light and vigor of oriental idealism like a feeble Promethean spark in the full heavenly glory of the noonday sun, faltering and feeble and ever ready to be extinguished."

Max Muller, the great German teacher of Orientalism, said, "The Bedanta has a unique character; unique compared with every other philosophy of the world which has not been influenced by it, directly or indirectly. None of our

The Nandi Bull, mystical vehicle of the great Lord Shiva. This enormous bull, chiseled out of a single rock, is in the Brihadeshwar Temple in Tanjore, South India. It is one of the largest carved bulls in India. The exquisitely carved pillars supporting the canopy depict mythical beasts.

philosophers, not excepting even Heraclitus, Plato, Kant, or Hegel, has ventured to erect such a spire, never frightened by storms or lightning. Stone follows upon stone, in regular succession, after once the first step has been made, after once it has been clearly seen that in the beginning there can have been but One, as there will be but One in the end, whether we call it Atman or Brahman."

Sir William Jones said, "It is impossible to read the Vedanta, or the many fine compositions in illustration of it, without believing that Pythagoras and Plato derived their sublime theories from the same fountain with the Hindu sages."

Schopenhauer said, "There is no study more beneficial to mankind than the study of the Upanishads. It has been the solace of my life, and it will be the solace of my death."

Such is the respect given the ancient wisdom of India by some of the greatest minds of our times, esoteric teachings worthy of our complete admiration and most careful study.

The "Vedas" are the revered Hindu Sacred Books dating back thousands of years. Some of the Vedas such as the Rig-Veda, the Yajur-Veda, and the Sama-Veda are devoted to Hindu religion and philosophy. The *Atharva-Veda* deals with quite another and different line of teaching, and while emanating from the same general source, it has been styled "The Veda of Magic Powers," and is instructive in the development of supernormal mental faculties, senses, and powers. There is mention made of both the high and low use of these powers;

the teaching ranges from the highest form of psychic power to the lowest form of witchcraft, sorcery, and black magic. The books composing this Veda are some twenty in number and contain recipes, formulas, rites, ceremonies, and performances for the production of psychic phenomena, magical ceremonies, invocations, evocations, enchantments, etc.; they exceed in variety and detail the better known similar writings of the ancient Hebrews and Greeks, and show with remarkable clearness how far the human mind may proceed along these lines.

Much of the high magic teaching of India has never been committed to writings by the ancient teachers, and their instruction has been carefully transmitted from teacher to pupil along many generations, over thousands of years.

In this book, I shall not attempt to set forth the philosophical teachings of the Hindus, but will devote attention entirely to instruction in the real magic of India as it is taught by oriental masters.

I open this text with a presentation of the conjuring feats of the Hindu fakirs, which the tourists see, and teach you their modus operandi. This magic is interesting, mystifying, entertaining, and is little known as it is traditionally passed down from father to son; the secrets of Hindu legerdemain being preserved within certain families. The fakir magic is knowledge that you should have, as it will serve to introduce you gradually to the true magic of the Adepts; which you will explore in this book as you plunge into an in depth study of oriental wisdom and learn of the control of the laws of nature by the hidden powers of the human mind which is the real magic of India.

Ron Ormond receives a copy of the Hindu Sacred Vedas from Swami Satish Chuttar.

HYPNOTISM AND MYSTICISM OF INDIA

India's doorway to mystery at Mysore. Enter through this fantastically carved ivory 18th Century door into the Land of Magic.

1
Hindu Fakir Magic

The magic of the fakirs is entirely an imitation of the real magic, in which the oriental conjuror plays the role of a magician and mystifies his audience with clever trickery. Hindu magic has an aura about it different from conjuring found in any other part of the world, as in being the imitation of the genuine, it preserves a certain earthiness (relationship to nature) which is found in the performance of the real magic.

In the first book of this trilogy, *The Secret World Of Witchcraft* (pub. A.S. Barnes and Co., Inc. 1973), I wrote of a typical fakir exhibition of magic as the tourist sees it frequently performed in India. This description and occasional other references are presented here with permission:

"While traveling in India, I saw the Hindu fakirs perform magic in many places; turbaned fakirs with bushy black beards on the street corners and in the parks, making balls leap cleverly from cup to cup, then suddenly transforming them into baby chicks.

"In a park not far from the Great Eastern Hotel in the heart of downtown Calcutta, I saw the 'Hindu Basket Trick' performed. The bearded magician placed a boy in a basket that seemed scarcely large enough to hold him, then forced down the lid. Picking up a sword, he ran it through the basket in many directions. What happened to the boy? The crowd was tense. Next the magician picked up a cloth and threw it over the basket; reaching beneath he removed the lid. Then he leaped directly into the basket, pulling the cloth inside with him. There was nothing there; the boy was gone! The magician jumped out, discarded the cloth, and replaced the lid on the basket. Suddenly he pointed, picked up the cloth, and advanced toward the crowd. The spectators gasped, because he appeared to grasp a struggling form beneath the cloth. He brought it back to the basket; the lid popped off, and there sprang up, alive and happy, the boy who had vanished.

"It was a beautiful illusion. Other tricks of fakir magic were now performed such as the classical 'Mango Tree Trick' and 'The Diving Duck.' Even though such feats were not the *real* mysticism and magic of India which I sought, as an

15

The incredibly magnificent Itma-Ud-Daulah of Agra, India. It is the first Moghul building designed entirely of white marble as the tomb of the grandfather of Mumtaz Mahal, the empress for whom the Great Taj was built. A two-storied structure, beautifully proportioned, it has mosaics with semi-precious stone inlay covering almost the entire surface. Inside are translucent marble screens hand carved so intricately, they appear like lace work.

American magician I, as did the spectators, appreciated the artful presentation greatly. The fakirs are very clever conjurors."

I will now share the secrets of Hindu conjuring with you. It is well that you understand such, as you will then appreciate the real magic even more.

While the feats performed by Hindu fakirs are numerous, I will describe the most popular and will designate them by their common names, which in most cases are very apropos. Let us begin with the famous "Mango Tree Trick." As the trick is usually performed, it is shown in this manner:

The fakir comes forward, almost nude, being covered only with a loin

16

The country fair at Pushkar. Here far out in the country some eleven kilometers from the city of Ajmer in Rajasthan, a lively fair is held in the fall of each year. There are camel races and all manner of amusements for the crowds who attend. To fairs such as this come the cleverest of the fakirs to amuse and amaze the natives with phenomenal exhibitions of magic.

cloth. It is obvious to the spectators that he has nothing concealed upon his person. As the trick is performed out-of-doors, the impromptu occasion demands no deceptive preparations. The fakir carries in his hands a little earthen pot containing water, and another containing a quart or so of dry sand. He also has with him some seeds of the mango-tree, and a large cloth, about four feet square. This is shaken out, and both sides are shown to the spectators, so that they may see nothing is concealed in the cloth.

All this having been gone through, the fakir proceeds to build a little mud pile of earth and water dexterously moulding them into a pyramid. The mango seed is now inserted in this soil, and covered on all sides with the earth. The fakir then constructs a little tripod of bamboo sticks and surrounds this with a shawl making a miniature tent; under this he works. He places his hands and arms under the shawl, manipulating the seed and earth for sometime. As his hands and arms are bare and can be seen never to approach his body, no deception is detected in this handling of the seed and earth beneath the cloth. After a few minutes of this manipulation, the fakir withdraws his hands, and proceeds to make passes over the little tent, at the same time muttering semiarticulate incantations. Sometimes a native drum is beaten, or other instrument is played upon, and, after a while, the fakir removes the cloth, and the seed is seen to have sprouted a couple of tiny leaves appearing above the surface of the earth.

Should the specators be skeptical, the fakir will remove the seed, and shows a couple of minute roots sprouting from the lower end of it. The seed is then replaced in the earth, the manipulations and incantations repeated, and, after awhile, the fakir removes the cloth a second time, and the mango is seen to have sprouted still more—now being several inches in height. This process is repeated five or six times, at the end of which period the mango-tree is two feet or more in height. Also on some occasions, the tree has been known to bear fruit.

Such is the effect of the trick as the spectators see it. Now for the explanation.

In the first place, it will be noted that it is always a mango-tree that is made to grow, and no other shrub. Why is this ? Surely it is not because the mango is the only tree in India that is ready to the hand of the fakir, for we know that there are numerous others that might be made to grow. Yet it is always the mango! I asked a Hindu fakir if he would make a young palm, a tea plant, or a banana tree grow for him, and received the response, "Nay sahib, cannot do. Mango-tree the only one can make." I repeat, why is this?

The reason is that owing to the peculiar construction of the mango leaf the trick is made possible. The leaf and twigs of the mango-tree are exceedingly tough and pliable, almost like leather, and can be folded or compressed into a very small space without breaking the stems or leaves, and, when this pressure is released, the leaves will resume their former expanded condition very rapidly, without showing any traces of the folding process. The leaves can be turned upon themselves and rolled into a tight ball, in which folded condition they occupy very little space, and yet will resume their extended condition when this pressure is released. This advances to the heart of the secret of the trick.

The mango seed that is placed in the mounded pyramid of earth is specially prepared before the performance, by the fakir, in the following manner:

He splits the seed open, scoops out its contents, dries it somewhat, then places within it a shoot of a mango-tree folded and pressed so as to fit inside neatly. It must be remembered that the mango seed is about two inches long by an inch and a half broad, so there is ample room for this preparation. It resembles slightly the mussel shell found on the seashore. It will be obvious that a seed of this size has space for containing a good deal of material, and if the mango leaves were folded in a small compass, the seed would hold a good-sized plant. The leaves are folded very carefully in a special manner. The upper surface of the leaf must be folded on itself, and that surface properly treated with water will scarcely show a crease on a superficial examination.

When the fakir places his hands beneath the cloth the first time, he then gets hold of the seed, and proceeds to manipulate it in such a manner as to extract from the upper end of the seed about an inch or so of the plant it contains. He may extract the seed altogether from the dirt for that purpose, and replace it in the earth again at the conclusion of this manipulation, banking up the earth around the seed before removing his hands. The fakir then removes his hands, and proceeds with the drumming and incantations as he sees fit to impress the onlookers. After a while, the cloth is removed and the seed is found to have sprouted, and an inch or so of the stem and the first green leaves are seen to be sprouting from the earth.

Hindu magicians and changra of the Punjab. These entertainers of Northern India are among the most expert of Hindu fakirs, combining clever conjuring with the secret knowledge. This group is appearing at the "Festival of Baisakhi" celebrating the beginning of the Hindu solar new year.

The illusion is perfect, and the spectators are more taken up with gazing in wonder at the miraculous growth and discussing it with each other than with critically examing the seed and the sprouting plant. If the fakir wishes to show the roots sprouting from the lower end of the seed, he merely has to place these roots in the seed before the performance begins, and extract them in the course of his manipulation of the seed, as previously explained. The preparation of the seed is concealed by the fact that a duplicate seed is first exhibited to the spectators and is examined by them. This seed is deftly exchanged for the prepared seed by the Hindu magician, and the latter seed placed in the ground. Thus, no one thinks of examing the seed after the performance is concluded.

To return to the performance of the trick, after the fakir has shown the growth from seed the first time, he covers the seed again with the cloth and places his hands underneath it. He works out a little more of the mango; then repeats his incantations, finally showing the shoot a second time, when it is found to have grown a considerable amount in the interval. Amazement stuns the group! The performance is gone through several times, until the folded mango shoot is all worked out of the seed, the growing plant being covered each time by the shawl. When the shoot is all worked out of the seed, there is a fair sized plant standing before the spectators.

This is but the beginning of the trick, some subtle business is now applied that completes the effect into a development of a mango tree standing several feet, and in some cases even bearing fruit. The secret is that Hindu fakirs seldom travel singly, but always in troupes of threes and fours. During the performance these others assist him by passing him the articles used in his performance, such as jars, water, earth, etc. Now, every time the East Indian conjuror moves the shawl from the growing plant, he tosses it to his assistant, and shows his hands empty. When receiving the shawl back from his assistant, he again shows his hands empty and shakes out the shawl and exhibits both sides of it proving in this way that nothing is concealed in the shawl. To all appearances, nothing could be fairer, but the fakir shows the shawl more casually each time, until towards the climax of the trick he hardly shows it at all. The spectators, having seen it empty so many times, get into the habit of thinking it is empty as a matter of course, and pay no attention to this part of the performance after the first few times. Their thoughts and attention are centered upon the mango-tree and its growth. So, when the conjuror has worked out all of the shoot from the seed, he is now ready for the introduction of a plant of larger size. To secure it unbeknown to the watchers, he gives a secret cue to his assistant that he is ready for the new "load," and the assistant in passing back the shawl to him this time passes him another cloth of similar type to the first. This second cloth is double, and contains a large mango plant, more or less doubled up in the manner of the first shoot that was placed within the mango seed. A slit in the cloth enables the conjuror to extract this folded plant, and place it in the mound of earth, working this plant out to its natural size with his hands beneath the cloth. When this large plant is worked out to its full size it makes a big display, and the fakir has only to remove the cloth to show the plant to his astonished onlookers.

The cloth just employed is exchanged for the original while the eyes of the spectators are fascinated by the huge tree just exhibited to them, and when the trick is concluded this cloth is handed for examination. Of course, no trickery is discovered in connection with the cloth. When it is desired that mango fruit be grown upon the tree, these are simply removed from a secret pocket in the cloth and are hung on the limbs amongst the leaves; the fruit is detached and handed to the spectators to eat before the surreptitious attachments can be examined. The whole performance is an excellent example of the psychology of deception—East Indian Style.

In what is known as "The Hindu Basket Trick," the effect of which I described in the beginning of this chapter, the fakir makes use of a large, oval basket, peculiarly constructed in being much larger at the bottom than it is at the top. These baskets are conventional in India, the lid being perhaps thirty inches by eighteen inches, while the central diameter of the basket spreads to about four feet seven inches, and then tapers down to approximately two feet six inches at the bottom. The basket's size, of course, can vary. Roughly, a basket of this design resembles a huge egg, with an opening on one side.

The basket is shown empty to the audience, and, as I mentioned in describing the effect, a boy is brought forward and stands in the basket. He is usually dressed in conspicuous clothing, such as a scarlet turban and jacket. He is placed in the basket, into which he apparently just fits, occupying the whole of it. The lid is placed upon his head, and a large cloth is thrown over it, completely covering him and the basket. He is seen to sink down gradually until he finally disappears into the basket altogether, and the lid resumes its natural position over the opening.

The performer now removes the cloth and proceeds to run the basket through and through with a sword. The basket is thoroughly pierced in this manner, and it appears as though the boy must be killed, even if somehow he managed to conceal himself within it. The fakir now replaces the cloth over the basket, places his hands under the cloth and removes the basket lid, throwing it to one side. He then places his hand into the basket and removes the scarlet turban and jacket, which he tosses out. The boy has apparently disappeared! To make matters more certain, the conjuror suddenly jumps right into the basket, stamps about with his bare feet, and ends by sitting in its himself.

As it was formerly seen that the basket was only large enough to contain the boy, it seems impossible that he can be concealed in or about the basket. The fakir then places the turban and jacket in the basket, replaces the lid and removes the cloth. Suddenly he darts forward, carrying with him the cloth, and snatches in the air with the cloth as if catching a body, and goes back with much excitement and much jabbering to the basket, which he covers with the cloth; when surprisingly something is seen to be moving under the cloth! Immediately the lid of the basket goes up. In another moment, the boy, clad in his jacket and turban, emerges from the basket, none the worse for his recent trying experience.

I shall now explain this apparent marvel.

The instant the boy is covered with the blanket he proceeds to divest himself of his jacket and turban, which he deposits in the bottom of the basket.

He now gradually sinks into the basket until he is completely inside it and the lid is even with the top of the basket. Now comes main portion of the trick—the method of concealment of the boy within the basket—for he does not escape from within it, but remains in it throughout the performance. It will be remembered that the lower portion of the basket is much larger than the top portion. The boy within the basket manages to so curl his body around the basket, eel-wise, that he is occupying the entire outer rim of the basket, so to speak, thus leaving the center of the basket (the part of the basket directly under the opening) empty. When the fakir runs his sword through the basket he takes pains to run it through this unoccupied space; and, by the concealed boy wriggling from place to place within the basket, the magician is enabled to run his sword through every portion of the basket in turn, and so give the appearance of its complete emptiness. It will now be seen that the fakir can place his hand inside the basket and remove the discarded jacket and turban; also the lid, and to stamp and sit in the basket, since the space he occupies is that left *unoccupied* by the boy in the basket. So long as the cloth is over the opening in the basket, the boy can never be seen.

The fakir then replaces the jacket and turban in the basket, and replaces the lid—all this before removing the cloth. As soon as the lid is again placed upon the basket the boy inside slips on his jacket and turban, and is ready to emerge from the basket as soon as the lid is withdrawn. The snatching in the air with the cloth is to distract the attention of the spectators away from the basket while the boy is donning his clothes. The cloth is then brought back to the basket, and the boy reappears.

There is also a version of "The Hindu Basket Trick" in which the boy disappears from the basket and appears in a tree-top. The effect in this form is an excellent example of the clever misdirection used by the fakirs.

To perform the trick in this manner, the basket is placed within a few feet of some convenient wall, and the trick is performed on that spot. Matters proceed very much as before until the time comes for causing the boy to vanish and reappear in the tree. When this time comes the fakir brings forward four poles, four or five feet in length, and these are stuck in the ground around the basket. The audience is in front of the basket, and the conjuror has two or three confederates stationed on each side of the basket. While in the basket the boy wraps up his turban and jacket in a cloth, and this the conjuror manages to get hold of and pass out to one of his assistants earlier in the trick, while the basket is being repeatedly covered and uncovered.

Presently the Hindu performers begin to quarrel among themselves, and, at the same time, others begin to play upon drums, etc. making an awful noise and distracting the attention of the spectators away from the basket containing the boy. Meanwhile, the fakir has procured a large strip of cloth, and has attached an end of this to one of the poles, the one nearest the onlookers. He then proceeds to attach it to each of the other four in turn, thus enclosing the basket in a roofless tent, the front side—the side nearest the audience—being enclosed last. At least, so it appears. What has really happened, however is this:

At the moment when the noise was created, and the conjuror's assistants began quarrelling among themselves, and the spectators' attention was accordingly distracted, the fakir crosses in front of the basket for a moment, as though to see what is the cause of the disturbance, and for an instant conceals the basket from view. In that instant the boy leaps from the basket, darts between the legs of one of the assistant helpers, and is lost behind them before the cloth strip is withdrawn that has concealed his escape. The entire action is performed so swiftly that no one notes it, especially as the observers were distracted by the noise and confusion, at that instant. The careful enclosure of the basket subsequently tends to convey the impression that the boy is still within it. He has now escaped, and is behind the nearby wall, thus hidden from the view of the spectators. He carries with him the cloth containing his turban and jacket, which he proceeds to don. Then, climbing a near-by tree, he is ready to cry out to the audience whenever he receives the signal from the fakir to do so.

Another popular effect of Hindu fakir magic is named "The Dry Sand Trick." In this case, the East Indian conjuror brings forward a little pail, some eight or nine inches high, and perhaps six inches across the top. This the fakir proceeds to fill with water. There is no trick about the pail, and the water is ordinary water, which may be supplied from any source. The conjuror next extracts a handful of dry sand from a bag and blows it hither and thither, showing it to be exceedingly dry. A portion of this sand is then carefully deposited in the bottom of the pail, in the water, and everyone can see it. The conjuror carefully washes and wipes his hands, and shows them perfectly clean and empty. Then, placing his hand in the water, he extracts from the pail a handful of the sand and shows it to be just as dry as when it was placed in the water. Blowing sharply into his hand, the sand flies in every direction, it is absolutely powdery.

This is a very ingenious trick, and could never be discovered unless its secret were explained. There is no trick about the pail or water, as stated; it all consists in the preparation of the sand. In order to prepare this sand for the experiment, the magician procures some fine, clean sand. This is washed carefully a number of times in hot water, so as to free it from any adhering dirt of any sort. It is then carefully dried in the sun for several days.

About two quarts of this sand is then placed in a frying pan and a lump of fresh lard (or parafine may be used) the size of a walnut is placed into the pan with it. This mixture is now thoroughly cooked over a hot fire until all lard is burned away, the result being that every little grain of sand is thoroughly covered with a slight coating of grease (or wax), which is invisible to the sight and touch, and, at the same time, renders the sand impervious to water.

When a handful of this treated sand is placed into the bucket of water, to be shortly again brought out, it is squeezed tightly together into a little lump, the grease making it adhere. Thus, when it is brought out it is quite as dry as when placed within the pail, and the Hindu fakir's magic is complete.

There is a trick similar to the one before popular in India, called "The Colored Sugars Trick." In this, the fakir eats a small quantity of sugar of different colors (black, red, yellow, green, and blue, along with the usual white sugar; it is easy to tint the sugars with harmless food dies). The various colors of sugar is chewed and swallowed by the conjuror, each in turn. The fakir then asks his audience to select whichever color they prefer of those swallowed, and, upon the choice being made, the conjuror immediately blows from his mouth the

Ron Ormond photographs the Fakirs in action.

colored sugar requested. This is repeated until all the colors have been called for in turn.

To accomplish this trick, the fakir has secretly prepared beforehand six small packages, each containing one of the colored sugars. These are enclosed in thin, parchment-like skin, and are secreted in the conjuror's mouth, three in each cheek, in a prearranged order. The fakir can easily reach any of these packets with his tongue, bring it to the front of the mouth, break the skin by pressing it against his teeth, and blow the sugar out in a perfectly dry condition. This is repeated until all six colored sugars have been produced.

If some skeptical specator wishes to examine the fakir's mouth, he merely swallows the skins. Hindu fakirs frequently swallow far more disagreeable things than skins for the sake of a few rupees on occasion. The colored sugars were also swallowed in the first place.

"The Diving Duck" is a puzzling bit of Hindu conjuring. The fakir sets a shallow bowl upon the ground, which he proceeds to fill with water. When this is done, the conjurer places a miniature artificial duck in the water, and then moves to one side and plays upon his flute. Soon the duck begins to move, and shortly dives beneath the water in a very natural manner. Whenever the hand of one of the spectators approaches near it, the duck dives out of sight, reappearing as soon as the hand recedes. Finally, the duck is taken out of the water, and immediately handed for examination; it is found entirely free from trickery of any sort. The bowl is also emptied of its water, and again shown to the onlookers.

The secret is this:

In the bottom of the shallow bowl there is a tiny hole bored, and through this is passed a thread or hair. To the inner end of this hair is attached a small dab of wax (sticky substance). The other end extends along the ground, and the

24

trick is always performed on soil the color of which makes the hair invisible. The duck is fastened to the inner end of the hair by means of the wax; and it can be readily seen that when the bowl is filled with water, the duck will dive beautifully every time the hair is pulled by the conjuror, and will rise to the surface when this pressure is released.

That is the complete secret of "The Diving Duck Trick." In order to conceal the fact that the bowl leaks, the conjuor first sprinkles some water on the ground, or fills the bowl so full (apparently by accident) that it overflows. This conceals the fact that water is gradually running out through the small hole in the bottom of the pot.

In another trick sometimes exhibited, the reverse method of "The Diving Duck" is employed. This Hindu trick is called "The Jumping Rabbit" in which a small toy rabbit placed in the water jumps out of the bowl and lands beside the bowl. No thread or hair is used in this case, and spectators sometimes come right up to the pail and stand over it while the rabbit makes his marvelous leap. The fakir may be any distance from the pail of water at the time, and even held by onlookers to prevent any action on his part.

The conjuror begins by filling the little pail with water. After he has done this he pours into the water some sand, and stirs it up with a stick. The sand muddies the water and makes it opaque. In the act of pouring in the sand and stirring the water, the fakir secretly introduces into the pail a thin but broad spring, bent over so as to form an almost complete circle. The two ends of the spring are kept apart by means of a piece of sugar; so that, when this sugar melts, the spring will be released and will spring open with a sudden jerk. It is upon this spring that the little rabbit is placed. The conjuror goes through the various incantations of playing on the drum, etc. until the sugar melts, when the spring will fly uncoiled, and the little rabbit jumps forth.

A Hindu Fakir version of "The Levitation" illusion. Lying flat on the ground, the body of the magician is covered with a cloth; he then rises high into the air. (Courtesy The Great Virgil Collection)

Ending the trick, the fakir turns the pail upside down allowing the water to escape and palms away the spring in his hand during this action.

Speaking of "palming" brings to mind a couple of East Indian sleight-of-hand tricks which I have seen. One is called, "The Beans and Scorpion Trick."

In this trick, three beans are changed into a scorpion. In the performance, the fakir has a box containing two compartments. In the upper one the beans are kept, while the lower compartment contains the scorpion. These compartments are separate, and either can be opened as desired. The fakir puts the three beans into the hand of one of the audience, and tells him to hold them. He then asks the spectator to open his hand again to see if they are still there. Of course they are, so the conjuror takes them out of this person's hand and puts them back in the box. He then asks the spectator to again hold his hand out; and, when he has done so, the conjuror deftly opens the lower box and allows the scorpion to fall into his hand, where he palms it. Thus the scorpion is dropped into the person's hand instead of the expected beans. The trick invariably causes much excitement.

Some species of scorpions found in India are harmless, but the creatures look vicious. The effect on the spectators is startling.

The second sleight-of-hand trick I wish to mention, is named, "The Basket and Chickens Trick." In this, the fakir exhibits a basket, some eighteen inches in diameter and twelve inches high. A stone is placed under the basket, which is then inverted over it. Soon the basket is lifted, and a snake or scorpion is found beneath it, while the stone has disappeared. The creature is thrown into a bag which the conjuror carries with him, and the basket is placed on the ground. After some more manipulation the basket is again raised, and this time some ten or fifteen little birds walk out from beneath it. Apparently nothing could be more extraordinary!

The explanation lies that in the act of inverting the basket the first time, the fakir introduces the scorpion and removes the stone by sleight-of-hand. The little birds are all contained in a black cloth bag, and are secretly introduced into the basket when every one's attention becomes centered on the appearance of the scorpion. That scorpion is the Hindu magician's misdirection, and very effective misdirection it is, as people instinctively back away from what is regarded as a poisonous creature.

In the action of the trick, as the inverted basket is raised the first time, and while all attention is upon the scorpion, the conjuror simply brings the basket back towards himself and loads the bag of chicks from beneath a bundled cloth lying by his side. It is but the act of a second to make this steal. The basket with the concealed bag of birds beneath is now placed in the center of the ground. The fakir places his hand underneath the inverted basket and releases the little chickens from the cloth bag. The little birds are free to scamper about, and when the basket is again lifted are a great surprise. The bag can be disposed of at any convenient moment.

One of the most surprising tricks of Hindu fakir magic I have ever witnessed was this one in which a magician took a little ball of rough cotton thread, and threw the ball to a woman who formed one of the party assisting him. She unravelled about two yards of the thread and broke it off. The fakir then took the thread and placed an end of it in his mouth, and by a deep breath the cotton flew into his mouth and he appeared to chew it. Then he borrowed a penknife from me, and with the big blade made as though he would stab himself in the throat, the woman preventing him with some show of excitement; but, presently, turning her back, the man seized the opportunity to plunge the knife into his stomach, and that he did very well. He then put his hand under the loose linen shirt he was wearing and began to draw out the length of cotton thread.

When he had drawn out nearly as much as the length of the piece which he had swallowed, he lifted his shirt slightly and showed the end of the cotton apparently embedded in the skin. He then took the knife and moved it upward against the skin as if he were pressing out the last bit of thread, which was tinged with blood.

I practiced the trick.

The sucking in of the cotton thread takes skill, but you can achieve it. The only precaution to be taken is to prevent the end coming into contact with the back of the throat, for if it does it will bring on an attack of coughing.

The plunging of the knife into the stomach is all pretense, and, of course, the chewing of the thread is merely a way of secreting it, as it is wadded into a small ball by the tongue, and is deposited between the side of the lower teeth and cheek. The piece of thread that is reproduced is another length of cotton rolled up beneath the shirt, the Hindu then makes a small nick in his skin and forces the end of the thread into this, the slight bleeding coloring the end of the thread. Thus it seems that following the pulling out of the thread, when the shirt is raised, the last bit of thread appears to be coming still out through a slit in the skin. In my performance, I got away from the cutting of the skin by merely fastening the end of the thread to the skin of the stomach with a bit of flesh colored tape of about a quarter of an inch size. This looks exactly as though the thread were sticking out of the skin, and the upward movement of the knife scraps this off, and the thread is pulled free. A little red coloring on the end of the string completes the illusion.

"The Brass Bowl Trick" is an ingenious effect performed by the fakirs. The Hindu magician brings forward a brass bowl which he shows empty. He fills this with cold water, placing a piece of ice in the water to emphasize that it is really cold. He then covers the bowl for a few moments with a borrowed handkerchief, makes passes over the bowl, plays on his drum, etc., and soon removes the handkerchief. The water in the bowl is now found to be scalding hot!

The secret of this astonishing trick lies in the peculiar construction of the brass bowl. The sides of the bowl are double, as are also the feet upon which it stands. When brought forward the space between the two sides of the vessel is filled with the boiling water, while the lower space is empty. While covering the bowl with the handkerchief, the faker has an opportunity to scratch off a wax pellet covering an air-hole, this allows the cold water to run down into the empty space in the foot of the bowl. By scratching off a second wax pellet on the side of the bowl, the hot water is made to run into the body of the bowl, until it finds its own level. The trick is a clever adaption of physics by the native East Indian magician.

27

Snake charming is commonly seen performed by the fakirs in India. While not conjuring, it is closely associated with the performances of these interesting magicians. The snake charming is genuine and is a skill acquired by long practice. Usually the cobra is used for this purpose, and being known as a deadly snake fascinates the watchers. Of course, the fangs of the serpents have been extracted, so it is not as dangerous as it seems. The Hindus are exceedingly dexterous in extracting fangs.

One of the classical feats of the Hindu fakirs about which stories have been circulated all over the world is that known as "Voluntary Interment."

In this demonstration, the fakir places himself in a self-induced trance (undoubtedly closely akin to self-hypnosis), he is then placed inside of a coffin, the lid nailed on. The coffin is then lowered into a grave and is covered with dirt. Sometimes no coffin is employed, the entranced fakir merely being lowered in a hole with boards placed over him before the dirt is heaped on top.

The fakir remains buried for an inordinate length of time, after which he is dug up, revived, and seems none the worse for his experience.

There is no trickery in the demonstration. A trance state is induced and the breathing and body functions reduced to a low ebb which makes it possible to survive for a surprisingly long time on the amount of air which exists in the burial situation. The feat is unquestionably dangerous, and many performances have resulted in death.

"The Voluntary Interment Trick," or as it is popularly called, "Buried Alive" is the most hazardous trick of Hindu Fakir Magic. So many magicians have been killed that the Indian government has now outlawed it being shown. In volume two of this trilogy, *Religious Mysteries of the Orient* (pub. A. S. Barnes and Co., Inc. 1975), I wrote of a personal experience with the effect in which my partner, Ron Ormond had a near brush with death. "The Buried Alive" performance, along with pain control feats such as sleeping on a "Bed of Nails," and passing pins through the flesh brings the fakir very close to genuine East Indian Magic about which I will write in the next chapter.

Ron Ormond, and "The Cobra Eating Magician." This Fakir performs the fantastic feat of swallowing a cobra alive. (Photos reprinted with permission from The Secret World of Witchcraft, *A. S. Barnes & Company, Inc. 1973)*

2

Genuine East Indian Magic

The real magic of India is of two types (1) "Illusionary Magic" in which the magician causes the effect to appear within the mind of the observer. This magic is related to hypnotism in its effect, but is caused, it is said, by a psychic process rather than a psychological one. *It is known as the intermediate magic.* (2) "Creative Magic" is the magic of the Masters in which the processes of nature are influence directly by creative mind. *It is known as the high magic.* Also, in the High Magic the Yogis place Astral Plane Phenomena in which are developed the extra sensory perception (ESP) powers of the magician. In this text, you will learn the secret techniques for the practice of these magics, as explained by Sadhu Parimal Bandu.

As I wrote in *The Secret World of Witchcraft*, the real magic of India is rarely found in the big cosmopolitan centers visited by the tourists, it is performed mostly in the back country for the native population. Thus, magic of this type is but seldom seen by western eyes, and one must probe deep into out-of-the-way places to find it. But it is there for the seeking. It is in such remote villages that a performance of the legendary "East Indian Rope Trick" may be found.

The performance of this fabulous illusion usually takes place in the open air, at a busy place in the village where a crowd will quickly gather. Believe me, a crowd can gather more quickly in India than in any place else in the world. It's like magic in itself. The magician takes his seat, squatting on the ground in what is called "the lotus position," with his knees out to the sides and his feet twisted into his lap. Then he enters at once into a state of intensified concentration.

The magician's assistants, seated at one side, now begin a crescendo of sound on cymbals and dull-sounding drums, producing a weird rhythmic cadence. Accompanied by this rhythm, the magician begins a slow, monotonous chant that produces a drowsy, hypnotic effect on the crowd. The words of the chant always seem to end in the syllable of "aum-m-m-m," resembling the drowsy hum of the bumblebee. Gradually, slowly but surely, a monotonous vibrating rhythm is created which is *felt* as definitely as it is heard by the spectators.

Wintertime in the northern village of Guimarg, Kashmir, India. In the smaller towns the searcher can witness some of India's most remarkable magic accomplished through the power of maya.

As a prelude to the performance, various tricks of the Hindu fakirs are now presented (such as you have previously read). This conjuring stirs the imagination of the witnesses, captures attention, and builds the crowd. The performance of "The East Indian Rope Trick" is about to begin.

Having completed his introduction of Hindu conjuring, and with a large crowd now assembled, the magician takes a sharp stick and draws a circle some twenty feet in diameter into the dirt of the ground. Those who wish to witness "The Rope Trick" are invited to stand within this circle. Many do, but there are always those who do not dare. The magician is now concerned only with those who stand within "the charmed circle" for they are to see a miracle of magic. He returns to his lotus position and while accompaning himself with his montonous chants begins rocking his body in circular motions of rotations from his hips upwards. In India they call this "the hypnotic sway;" it is performed in imitation of the cobra as it charms its prey. Strangely it grips the attention of the spectators within the circle, and they watch in silence. If one amongst them could but take his eyes free of the magician for but a moment, it would be seen that the crowd sways in unison.

Unfolding his feet, the magician slowly rises and taking a sizeable coil of rope which has been presented to him by an assistant, he swirls it through the air. As if suddenly gripped by an unseen hand from the sky, its end is pulled swiftly upward, and it hangs in midair suspended between heaven and earth. A muffled gasp is heard from the spectators.

The magician pulls upon the rope and it seems solidly supported in the air. As the muffled drumming continues, the magician motions to a boy in the crowd to come forward and climb the rope. Hand over hand the lad mounts the rope

In the back country where exhibitions of the real magic of India are found. Traveling down the lush waterways of the Kerala, one can go from one little town to the next seeking out some of India's great mysteries of magic.

until he finally straddles its tip high up in the sky. With a wave of his hand, the magician causes the boy to vanish from the top of the rope. The spectacle is beyond belief, and the spectators can but gaze in speechless awe.

The magician then calls upon the boy to reappear, but there is no response. He increases his demands, but to no avail. Then, grasping a sword, the magician, himself, climbs the rope. Arriving at its tip he disappears into thin air. Only the magically suspended rope is now seen by the witnesses, but shouts and cries of pain are heard from the atmosphere high above the upturned faces of the crowd.

Suddenly the severed arm of the boy drops from the sky above and falls to the ground. The crowd leaps back! Another arm quickly follows, then the severed right and left leg, the cut up torso of the boy and his mangled head drop to the ground. It is a gastly sight.

As mysteriously as he vanished, the magician reappears at the top of the rope and descends it to the ground. Aided by his assistants, the magician gathers up the dismembered portions of the boy's body and places the pieces in

31

A combination of England and India is observed in this magnificent structure, The Victoria Memorial. Located in Calcutta, it was built by the British Viceroy, Lord Curzon, during the reign of Queen Victoria. Designed entirely in marble, it attempts in one breath to suggest both St. Paul's Cathedral of London and the Taj Mahal of ancient Delhi.

a basket. The basket is placed beneath the suspended rope. With a clap of the magician's hands the rope drops into the basket and at the same moment, the boy stands up from same, alive, well, and his body perfect.

The remarkable "East Indian Rope Trick" is over.

Without question "The East Indian Rope Trick" is the world's most famous feat of magic. It is talked about, written about, and conjectured about, yet surprisingly it has been seen but by a very few outside of India, however those few world travellers are sufficient for it is a never-to-be-forgotten experience that stirs the imagination of everyone. With the performance of magic of such an amazing nature, it is to be little wondered that speculation has arisen asserting the audience must be hypnotized to see such an occurrence. I asked Parimal Bandu about this, he nodded slowly and said, "Yes, it is hypnotism of an oriental kind, but it is quite different from the psychological hypnotism you know in the west. In India, it is what we call 'maya.' "

I have mentioned maya in my previous books in this trilogy. Maya is indeed a type of hypnotism, but of a unique oriental type that is produced through the use of suggestion combined with the visualized and projected concentrated thought of the magician to conjure up illusions within the mind(s) of the spectator(s). Combined with crowd psychology, with it accompanying hynotic effects, the results are startling. It is this principle of maya which is much used by the intermediate magicians of India to produce their most effective magic.

To appreciate maya one must recognize that telepathy (which is only now being given serious study in the Occident) has been an accepted part of oriental psychology for centuries. Every English person, who has lived in India, knows of the native "mental telegraph" by which important news is transferred. The history of England's rule in India is filled with many instances of this. News and general information were flashed from one end of India to the other, even before the days of radio. Let there be an uprising, a rebellion, or even a minor disturbance in some remote and inaccessable corner of India, and, before the day is past, natives in other parts of the land, often thousands of miles away, will be found to be fully acquainted with the fact.

On tour in India, Virgil and Julie (The Great Virgil Show) performing a stage version of the legendary "East Indian Rope Trick."

Through long years of association with it, eastern people have become far more sensitive to telepathy than people of the west. There is a general mental attitude of the acceptance of extra sensory phenomena that seems to make the oriental mind most receptive to thought vibrations. The general sensitivity, developed over many centuries, produces in the masses a blending, fusing, or harmonizing of thought called "thought contagion." All crowds of people feel this, but the East Indian people are especially open to it.

What is more, it has been discovered that when crowds of people are gathered together a peculiar amalgamation of their respective mental activities occurs. Mental action and reaction within massed crowds, usually below the threshold of consciousness, produces an average mental attitude; the various individuals adopt this average attitude in place of their own. Crowds of people under this influence lose their individuality and respond to group psychology and manipulation.

My good friend Parimal Bandu in India explained this to me. A crowd of natives around an oriental magician soon respond to "thought contagion" and become submerged in the average mental atmosphere. This condition of psychic receptivity is greatly conducive to the success of the wonder worker.

In the production of this form of magic, Bandu told me, the magician employs the power of "concentrated visualization," energized by what is called "prana." By directing his will, the magician causes his mental images to project themselves as real to the vision of his audience. In this way, he produces an illusion—a form of which the Adepts call maya, whereby the senses of the observers report as fact things that have no real existence. In other words, the magician creates and projects a powerful and concentrated thought form, which to the observers seems temporarily to exist as reality. Here, at last, is the real secret of the famous "East Indian Rope Trick."

Telepathy has an important place in relation to oriental wisdom and you will learn more of using this maya as you delve deeper into the real magic of India.

It is held by the Hindu Sages that there is no magic that is supernatural. The supernatural belongs to the superstitious, while real magic is supernormal. In other words, magic is above and beyond the normal occurrences in nature but functions always in complete accordance with her laws. The Adepts instruct that there are three principles of nature which combined correctly are the source and power of all magic. They are, viz.: 1 Akasha, the etheral substance pervading all space, and from which all material forms are produced. 2 Prana, the subtle energy which animates and energizes all nature. 3 Creative Mind, the mental element in which all designs are created in imagined form, after which they become materialized in objective form through the action of visualization, accompanied by the action of prana operating upon the akasha which is the essential and original state of matter.

The western student will recognize in these three principles the basis of all created matter as observed by science, the akasha being the all prevading atomic material in space from which all matter is formed, the prana as the energy force (including life) which animates and energizes all things, and Creative Mind as the designer of matter, as is expressed so well in the phrase, "What is to be must first be created in the unreality of imagination before it can

34

Dal Lake Srinagar, the Kashmir center of magic. When you visit this beautiful and remote area, you can live in these little houseboats right on the lake. The houseboats can be moved from one part of the lake to another. Srinagar is the base for visiting the rest of the valley.

become material reality." In one particular instance however, eastern thought has advanced beyond western thought in that while the occident uses these factors in nature indirectly, oriental thought affirms they can be controlled directly by mind, and in that step forward we have magic. As this book deals in the oriental methods of using that magic, I will instruct you in the Yoga way. Accordingly, I will now outline each of these three basic principles in closer detail in order that you will understand this oriental wisdom and subsequently learn how to make use of these finer forces of nature.

The Principle of Akasha. In the Hindu teachings, it is held that there exists a universal material principle which is known as akasha. Akasha is the basis for all matter, yet it is not to be identified with matter in any of the forms by which we know it through our senses. Rather, it is the "subtle essence" from which all that we know and experience as matter is evolved and produced. It is held to pervade all space, and as such is omnipresent. It is taught that all forms of matter, from the rarest gasses to the most solid of metals are evolved from this subtle principle. Therefore, akasha is regarded as the essential base substance of all material things, from atoms to stars, from microscopic forms of life to man, and it may be molded and formed by Creative Mind through the agency of prana.

As such, it is the way that God, as the First Cause, created the Universe and all that is, and man as created in God's Own Image likewise has access to using this basic material for his own creations.

35

Akasha, in its original and elemental form, is held by the Yogi teachers to be undifferentiated, simple, ultimate, and without any of the qualities or properties manifested in its countless derivative forms which we know as matter. It is infinitely finer, more subtle, and more tenuous than any known form of matter—even the thinnest of gases; it is reported to pervade all space. It is held to be of "infinite thinness and rarity, subtleness and tenuousness." The finest gas or vapor is much more solid than it, as the most solid rock or metal is more solid than such gas or vapor. Its degree of fineness and nonsolidity is such as to be quite beyond the imagination of man. Akasha is held to be without life, mind, will, or consciousness, and to manifest the forms of these only under the influence of Creative Mind assisted by prana. To reiterate, as such, akasha becomes the infinite supply of basic material from which every material thing is formed in endless variety.

The Principle of Prana. In the Hindu teachings, it is held that there exists a universal principle of energy which is known as prana. Prana as the universal energy source is dual in nature, it being the source of all motion, all force, and all active power. Also, it is the source of all vital energy, or life force. As prana is the energy source for the performance of all magic, it is important that you understand it well. Here is what oriental scholars have to say on the matter:

Yogi Ramacharaka states, "Prana is the name by which we designate that universal principle which is the essence of all motion, force, or energy whether manifested in gravitation, electricity, magnetism, the motion of the planets, and in all the activities of life, and in all forms of life from the highest to the lowest. It may be called the *soul of energy,* and it also is the principle which, when operating in certain ways, causes that form of activity which distinguishes life. It is the active principle in life; it is the vital force. Prana is all pervading. It is found in all things having life, and as the ancient teaching is that there is life in everything in the universe (both animate and inanimate), in that sense everything is living.

"Prana is in all forms of matter, yet it is not matter. Prana is in all forms of mind, yet it is not mind. Prana is in the air, yet it is not air. Prana is in every breath, yet it is not breath. Prana energizes all things, yet it is not those things in themselves. We can best understand the concept of prana by thinking of it as living force, or, more properly still, as the essence and principle of living force."

Swami Vivekananda says, "The universe is manufactured from its subtle material (akasha) by the power of prana. Prana is the infinite, omnipresent manifesting power of the universe. At the beginning and end of its especial cycle every material substance is resolved into its elemental and most subtle state or condition; all the forces of the universe are resolved back into prana. Thus, out of this prana is resolved everything that we call force; it is prana that is manifesting as motion in the operation of all things in obedience to the physical laws of nature, and it is prana that is manifesting in the actions of the body as the nerve currents, as thought-force. From the highest forms of thought down to the lowest physical force, everything is the manifestation of prana.

"To achieve the subtle perception of the finer forces which are operating in the physical body, we must first commence with the grosser perception and understand that the force which is setting the whole machine in motion is that of

36

Fakirs learn magic at an early age. Here a child magician performs the feat of passing a trident through the tongue.

A Fakir thrust a knife through the neck of a child magician. Blood runs freely, but moments later the child is unharmed. (Courtesy The Great Virgil Collection)

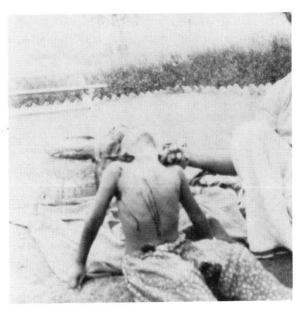

prana, the most obvious manifestation of which is the breath. Then, along with breath, we slowly enter the body, and are thus enabled to discover the subtle forces of the nerve currents which are moving all over the body. As soon as we discover the latter, and learn to feel them, we begin to get control of them which in turn gives us control over the body. The mind also is set in motion by these different nerve currents, so in our developing control of prana we ultimately reach the state where we have perfect control over the body and mind, and make both our servants. Knowledge is power, and we must first get this power by beginning at the beginning, and the beginning is the control of prana by means of Pranayama. Pranayama is the knowledge and control of prana.

"Pranayama opens to us the door of most remarkable powers. If one understood prana perfectly and could control it, every form of magic lies at his beck and call. He would be able to do all manner of amazing things, and be a magician of the highest sort. All because he would control prana. This is the aim of achievement in mastering Pranayama. When the magician becomes perfect in mastering prana, the finer forces of Nature will be under his control. When the uninformed see these powers they call them miracles, and the greatest miracle worker is he who has grasped prana as through it he grasps control of the finer forces of the universe both mental and physical. He who has control of prana has controlled his own mind, and the minds of others. He who has controlled prana has controlled his own body, and the bodies of others, because prana is the generalized manifestation of force."

The genuine Hindu magicians practice the methods of Pranayama, methods in which I will instruct you in this book, for the purpose of getting control of prana, and in direct ratio to the achievement of that control does one advance to the status of a Master.

And the control of prana has it purpose in matter of health as well, for by means of the control of prana is vitality increased, for prana is the creator and supporter of vitality. Prana exists in the atmosphere, and when one breathes into his lungs the air of that atmosphere he also breathes in prana. By means of certain Yoga methods, one can raise the degree of circulation of the prana in the blood and in the nerve currents and in the organs of the body bringing health and well being to the body. A detailed discussion and instructions for the application of these Yogi methods of health will be found carefully considered in relation to the practice of Yogi Therapeutics in *Religious Mysteries of the Orient* (pub. A. S. Barnes and Co., Inc. 1975).

The Yogis in their practice of Yoga are very interested in this health and healing phase of the magical powers. For such purpose, Yogis apply these same principles and direct them towards self-development and supernormal control of mind and body. The yogis function as the teachers, and their instructions take a variety of forms, which are designated as different types of Yoga.

The Principle of Creative Mind. In the Hindu teachings it is held that there exists a universal mental principle which is known as "Creative Mind." Its essence and elemental character may be described as being something like a blending or combination of imagination and will. Each individual is possessed of a portion of this Creative Mind, and is able to use it in the direction of visualization and projection upon the Material Principle (akasha) aided by the

A visit to Sonmarg, Kashmir, situated in the foothills of the Himalayas. Kashmir has been called "A PARADISE ON EARTH" at an elevation of nine hundred feet. Here in the Himalayas one can occasionally witness demonstrations of the high magic of India.

Energy Principle (prana) so as to *create* there in material form the reproduction of that which he has previously visualized in ideal form in his mind.

This Creative Mind Principle, present in man, is the instrument whereby he performs (consciously or unconsciously, for good or for harm to himself and others) his creative acts; it is the controlling instrument for the performance of all acts of genuine magic.

The Hindu teachings do not hold that this principle of Creative Mind is pure spirit, nor do they hold that it is identical with the ego or "I" of man. The "I" of the individual is held to be pure spirit (the soul) which is something over and above the mental faculties and instruments of expression. Accordingly, the Creative Mind is held to be entirely an instrument for the control of power as it is directed by the "I" of the individual. I will not attempt to follow oriental thought into the realm of pure spirit as it is outside the purpose of this volume of the trilogy. The student will find much on pure spirit manifestation discussed in *Religious Mysteries of the Orient*. Sufficient for the present consideration and instruction is to appreciate the self-evident fact that the individual "I" is the central essence and point of one's being, which he speaks of as *self*, from which proceeds all the physical and mental organs, parts, powers, talents, abilities, and faculties which are instruments or channels of expression and manifestation of his specific individuality. *Among these instruments of expression for each individual stands most importantly the one known as Creative Mind.*

The Creative Mind of Man, according to the Hindu teachings, as I have said, is a curious and interesting blending of the elements of imagination and will. The element of imagination, or "Image-Making," creates and produces the mental or ideal pattern upon and according to which the outward or objective form is reproduced and manufactured. The element of *will* serves to project and hold firmly fixed the ideal form visualized by the element of imagination, until upon and around it are deposited and formed the essential substance of the akasha, the material element from which all material forms and things are created and composed. In this process, the prana, or Energy-Principle is

employed in the creative work of manifesting the visualized ideal form as stated above.

In considering the elements combined in the Creative Mind Principle, the student must not fall into the error of thinking of the element of imagination as being that of mere fancy, or fanciful idle-thought thinking. Such idle fancying is but day-dreaming and is not the real essence of creative imagination. Creative imagination on the contrary, is the real constructive, inventive, designing, creative faculty of the mind. From it arise all great inventive work, all plans and designs, all artistic creations, in fact all models and plans and designs, all artistic creations, in fact all models and plans of things that are to be created and made into material reality. Also, it conceives the actual building processes by which such plans are carried out.

Creative imagination is thus seen as the great constructive and creative principle of the mind of man from which all of his achievements have developed, directly proceeding from the application of this inherent principle of his mentality.

As a portion of creative imagination belongs to each individual, obviously western people are no strangers to it. Indeed, creative imagination has been tremendously active in the Occident. One has but to look around at the many achievements in architectural masterpieces, inventions, even the conquest of space to instantly appreciate this. Every man-built structure is merely a material representation or reproduction of some man's or men's mental image. And every such mental image, design or plan that has ever been formed in the mind of man, was formed first in his creative imagination.

As commented, a unique point in which the oriental sages advance beyond western man in his creative use of imagination is in the premise that blended with will, it can create material representations of itself *directly* independent of the need for laborious physical proceedings of manufacturing. *In other words, the Hindu teachings hold that mind, when advanced enough, has the power of materializing physical creation directly itself*. The achievement of this is the aim of every magician, the skill is but rarily obtained except in advanced Adepthood, but it is said to be there as part of man's mental inheritance to be used when he evolves sufficiently to make use of this godlike ability.

The achievement of that power is the basis of *The High Magic of India and Tibet* (both of which are synonymous as many of the more advanced East Indian Sages seek the solitude of the high mountains in Tibetian monasteries for pursuing their studies) in which nature is directly controlled by mind. Sadhu Parimal Bandu presents a study of this high magic (which he termed The Sacred Magic of Tibet) in *The Secret World of Witchcraft*—see chapter twelve, pages 160-168.

The Hindu teachings inform us that all magic creations of any kind are first designed in the image-making faculty of imagination of the magician. The clearer and stronger such mental images, the stronger and clearer will be the effect produced in the form or activity reproduced in the physical world. Accordingly, they teach that in concentrated visualization (the formation of strong concentration upon mental pictures) is found the first step of the process of magical materialization. The Hindu mystics devote much study, great care, and time to cultivation of this power of concentrated visualization. By

Eleven thousand seven hundred and fifty feet in the Himalayas at the Kedamath Temple along the pathway trod by pilgrims yearly. Many Yogis join the travellers and proceed onward into the mountain vastness to the Tibetan monasteries to study the high magic.

employing the crystal ball for this purpose they acquire a marvelous proficiency in the skill; you will also be instructed in the skill.

The element of Will, when it is combined with imagination in Creative Mind is of obvious importance; it is the driving force of achievement. Will, according to the teachings of the Hindu Sages, is the instrument whereby the visualized picture of the magician is projected upon the askasha, and then held firmly there until the materialization is completed. In this process of projection certain techniques must be employed. These will be taught you in subsequent chapters of this volume.

The Hindu teaching informs us that the visualized mental-picture may be projected by the trained will to great distances in space. It is taught that an Adept may by "will projection" cause his visualized mental picture to appear in places as he wishes; there to materialize itself by mean of the employment of sufficient prana. The mental-picture so projected is then "held firm" by the will until the manifestation is complete. Distance is never any barrier to mind. This principle, in varying degrees of performance, is employed consciously or unconsciously, as the case may be, by every person performing any act of magical procedure, no matter under what name the process is applied and manifested. It is one of the basic processes for the operation of genuine magic.

In all works related to the real magic, one will find references made frequently to the human will and its powers, but very little instruction has ever been given as to how the will must be developed and trained to be properly used in such processes. You will be given this instruction. For the moment, just bear

41

in mind the fundamental fact that the will is employed to support and "back up" the visualized mental-image after having been employed to project the image toward the scene of its future activity. Such is the action of will in magic.

Imagination and will are "the magic twins" of the Principle of Creative Mind. When energized by prana such are drawn into the mind and nervous system of the magician to a powerful degree producing genuine East Indian Magic. Of such is the teachings of the oriental Masters.

You now have knowledge of the three types of magic of India, viz.: 1 Hindu Fakir Magic. 2 Illusionary Magic of Maya. 3 Creative Magic. You also have knowledge of the trinity of the sources of magical power, viz.: 1 Akasha. 2 Prana. 3 Creative Mind. Also, there is a fourth which is related to the third that pertains to the extra sensory powers of the magician. You will learn how to develop these powers for the performance of real magic.

As I glanced up from my notes, Parimal Bandhu looked directly at me and said, "Let me emphasize the importance of what I have told you by putting it in the words of the great teachers who exclaim, 'O, student, learn well of the basics of akasha, prana, and creative mind for such are the foundation stones for the performance of all magics.' "

3

The Science of Pranayama

First in learning of genuine East Indian Magic must be the cultivation of your mystic source of energy (prana), for it is prana that places *power* behind your magic. Prana provides that power in charging "the magic twins" of imagination/will with force. The Yogis have developed over centuries of study, certain methods of charging the mind and nervous system with prana through techniques of life-giving breath. This particular method of breathing, referred to by the master teachers as Pranayama (prana absorbing rhythmic breathing), is vital to the performance of magic. To this end, study the science of Pranayama as taught in the Orient. It is carefully mastered by all who would be magicians.

Pranayama in definition is the science of the regulation of breath for the purpose of controlling, directing, and applying the prana or vital/energy force. Pranayama is largely concerned with rhythmic breathing consisting of stages of inhalation, retention, and exhalation of the breath in prescribed rhythm. Pranayama is a feature of the great school of Yogi teaching known as Raja Yoga, and is regarded by Hindu Sages, as well as by their students, as a very important part of their magical instruction.

Before proceeding to instruct you in the precise technique of Hindu Rhythmic Breathing, I shall describe the Hindu teaching concerning the physical mechanism which is employed in the processes of Pranayama (the control of prana):

In addition to western physiological knowledge concerning the two great branches of the nervous system, viz., the cerebrospinal nervous system and the sympathetic nervous system, the Hindu Sages teach an additional knowledge concerning man's nervous system, a knowledge that has long been held secret. It is the knowledge known in India as Kundalini, "the serpent power."

For an understanding of this power, the Yoga teachings hold that in each human body there is stored up a supply of prana, and that this supply is constantly in touch with the universal supply of prana which abides throughout all space. Or, to phrase it in the quaint manner of the East, the human body is regarded as a little inlet of prana which is connected with the great ocean of prana, from which an infinite supply may be drawn.

The figurative illustration of the tiny inlet and the great ocean of prana, mentioned above, is part of a favorite Hindu philosophy. It aptly pictures the apparent separateness, but also shows the real connection of contact of the individual existence with the Universal Existence, and of the power which abides in each. In this the Yogi feel that he has "all the prana there is" to draw upon when he needs a greater supply; such is affirmed by the highest of oriental teaching.

Let us now take a general view of the Yoga teachings concerning the psychic/physical mechanism over and by means of which the prana operates in the process of Pranayama.

First, it is held that the spinal column is the seat of a wonderful arrangement which is still to be appreciated by western science. The spinal cord is regarded as having an invisible channel in its center called the *sushumna*. On either side of the sushumna flows a current of prana—the two currents passing through the substance of the spinal cord.

At the lower end of the sushumna (the base of the spinal cord) is found a subtle invisible substance, a tenuous form of akasha in the shape of a triangle. This triangular shaped substance is known as "the Lotus Chamber of the Kundalini," and is the reservoir or storage center of a certain very powerful form of prana which is called kundalini. Kundalini is often referred to as "the secret energy" or "the serpent power" in Hindu teachings. It is regarded as of the greatest importance, and is held as *the key of power* in many magical and occult processes.

The two currents of prana which flow along the channel of the spinal cord known as the sushumna have distinctive Hindu names. The current that flows on the right side being called *pingula*, and is the positive current. The current that flows on the left side being called *ida* (pronounced "ee-dah"), and is the negative current. The terms pingula and ida also apply to the respective channels over which these currents flow, as well as to the currents themselves. Each of these currents has its own distinctive qualities and properties, and produces its own effects. They also constitute important elements in the science of Pranayama.

Another important element of Pranayama is that of "the sushumna lotuses. These are great centers of prana which are located in certain positions along the channel of the sushumna. These "lotuses" or centers are as follows:

1   The Muladhara, or lowest lotus, located at the base of the spinal column.

2   The Svadhisthana, the second in ascending order, located on the spinal column in the region of the reproductive organs.

3   The Manipura, the third in ascending order, located on the spinal column in the region of the solar plexus.

4   The Anahata, the fourth in ascending order, located on the spinal column in the region of the heart.

5   The Visuddha, the fifth in ascending order, located on the spinal column in the region of the throat.

6   The Ajna, the sixth in ascending order, located on the spinal column in the region of the pineal gland within the head.

7 The Sahastrara ("the thousand petalled lotus"), the seventh and highest in ascending order, located at the top of the head (extending in astral form and substance even outside of the head and above it; as the Hindus express it, "brooding over the crown of the head like a bird over her nest".)

These seven centers (lotuses) are called in Hindu teachings *the chakras*. The term "chakra" in definition means wheel, disc, or whirling around object. This term is applied to these centers because the latter manifests a peculiar vibratory, whirling activity when aroused into motion by the kundalini ascending the channel of the sushumna. In addition to *the seven great chakras*, there are also various minor chakras located in various parts of the body, but these do not especially concern our present study.

The chakras are not physical organs of the nervous system but are psychical ones. In other words, they are composed of astral or etheric material. The Hindu teaching considers them as "psychic centers of power."

The Brihadesware Temple of Tanjore. Seen through the massive stone gateway is the gopuram of the temple, which towers to a height of 216 feet. The dome rests on a single granite block and is beautifully carved with human figures on the broad base of the tower. The Brihadeswara is known as the grandest temple in India. The building was begun by Emperor RAJA Chola in A.D. 895. It took more than a hundred years to complete the structure.

When not aroused and energized by the ascending kundalini, the masters say the chakras are motionless and rest like drooping flowers. However, when they are energized, they raise themselves like sunflowers facing the sun and their motionless condition is transformed into one of a rapid whirling motion.

As was mentioned, the function of the lowest chakra (the muladhara) is to act as the storehouse of the kundalini, that potent form of prana. It is the function of the highest chakra (the sahastrara) to distribute the kundalini to the brain. In its entirety, the sushumna may be considered as a great battery of psychic force and power, and each of its chakras has its own special function in

The enchanting Shore Temple, Mahabalipuram, India.

the generation and distribution of certain forms of prana within the nervous system.

Of such is the psychic/physiological system of these tenuous organs within the human body.

In Pranayma, the practice of the correct rhythmic breathing, there is set into action the forces of the sushumna and its associated chakras in the direction of arousing, releasing, and directing the kundalini or "serpent power." Thus by the oriental system of rhythmic breathing the magician releases and directs the potent kundalini according to his will, and in this process produces the *power* for his performance of the real magic of India.

Every person is the possessor of these psychic/physiological organs of power, and, as such, is a potential magician, but in the average individual the sushumna channel is almost entirely closed. It is in the degree of the psychic or occult development of the individual that this channel is opened, and, in direct ratio to that opening, is measured the magical abilities of the person. Despite some repetition, so important is this to your developing skill as a magician that I want you to have a description of this important psychic process in the actual words of the Hindu Sage, Sadhu Parimal Bandhu, exactly as I recorded them:

"In the lotus of the kundalini, there is the power of the kundalini coiled up. When that kundalini awakes, it tries to force a passage through that hollow canal running through the spinal cord called the sushumna. As it ascends the sushumna, the kundalini rises step by step, and, as it were, layer after layer of the mind becomes opened, and all the different powers of Yoga become manifested. When it reaches the brain, the Yogi becomes the master of mind and body. He finds himself free, and filled with power.

"In the rhythmic breathing of Pranayama comes a tendency of all the molecules of the body to flow in the same direction. And when mind changes into *will*, these currents change into a motion similar to that of electricity in exact manner that the nerves show polarity under the action of electric currents. For your understanding, this shows that will evokes within the nerve currents an action very similar to electricity. Indeed, it is intimately related to electricity.

"When all the motions of the body have become perfectly rhythmical, the body will have become, as it were, a gigantic battery of will. This is the true "will power." This tremendous will is exactly what the Yogi wants. In this is the physical explanation of the importance of the breathing exercises of the Yogis. They bring about a rhythmic action in the body, and help us, through the respiratory centers, to control other centers. Thus the aim of Pranayma here is to arouse the coiled-up power in the muladhara, which is called the kundalini.

"All the sensations and motions of the body are being sent to the brain, and sent out of it through the wires of the nerve fibres. The column of sensory and motor fibres in the spinal cord are the ida and pingala of the Yogis. They are the main channels through which the afferent and efferent currents are traveling. But why should not the mind send the news without any wires? Taking the analogy of electricity, we find that man can send a current only along a wire; but nature requires no wires to send her tremendous currents. Indeed, your western science will eventually find the means of transmitting electricity without wires. Mind can do it now. This proves only that the wire is not really necessary, but

The renowned Rameshvaram Temple at Rameswaram. The sacred town is built on an island in the Palk Straits and is about 420 miles from Madras. It is one of the most famous temples in all of India.

Interior view of the Rameshvaram Temple. The temple is especially noted for these long perambulatory corridors that aggregate to a length of four thousand feet.

that only our inability to dispense with it compels us to use it. The Yogis say that if the mind can send the news without the wires of the nerve fibres, then one has removed the bondage of matter.

"If you can make the current pass through the sushumna, you have worked the problem. The mind has made the network of the nervous system, and has to break it, so that no wires will be required to work through. Then alone will all knowledge come to us and there will be no more bondage of body; that is why it is so important to get control of the sushumna. If you can send the mental current through that hollow canal, without any nerve fibres to act as wires, the Adepts acclaim you have solved the problem, and it is also spoken that it can be done.

"The sushumna in average persons is closed up at its lower extremity, thus no action comes through it. The Yogis propose a practice by which it can be opened, and the nerve currents made to travel through it. The center where the residual sensation are, as it were, stored up, is called the muladhara which is the root receptacle within which is the coiled-up energe of 'the serpent power (kundalini)' ready for action when it is aroused. Now, if this coiled-up energy is aroused and made active, and then consciously by will made to travel up the sushumna canal, as it acts upon center after center (the chakras), a tremendous reaction will set in. And when it reaches the metropolis of all sensations, the brain, the whole brain will react, and the result is the full blaze of illumination.

"Whenever there has appeared any manifestation of supernormal power, magic, or wisdom, such inevitably must have been the result of some current (even if in small amounts) of the kundalini having found its way into the sushumna, for such is the power of all magic no matter what its form. Many such practices set free a minute portion of the coiled-up energy of the kundalini purely through happenstance. Only in the practices of the East Indian Masters in Yoga is the true potential realized."

As I have pointed out to you in this consideration of the science of Pranayama, the arousal of "the serpent power" is the great aim of the Yogis. Thus aroused, the kundalini ascends and mounts in spiral movement like the wriggling of a snake, upward along the channel of the sushumna. Until aroused, the kundalini is a sleeping serpent which remains coiled-up and inert. It is not dead, however, but merely sleeping or hibernating like a snake during winter. It remains static until aroused into dynamic action by the proper methods or stimuli.

There are several reasons for the kundalini being called "the serpent power" by the Hindus. In the first place, the "coiled-up" position of the inactive kundalini is akin to that of the serpent. Again, the "wriggling motion" of the ascending kundalini, in its spiral mounting of the sushumna, closely resembles that of the moving serpent. In its dormant, sleeping state, the kundalini is sometimes represented by the familiar occult symbol of the serpent holding its tail in its mouth, or having swallowed its tail.

In this symbolic representation, however, the Hindus have no intention of ascribing an evil character to the power in showing it as a serpent. On the contrary, they employ the serpent as a symbol of wisdom and power, and it is abundantly active in high states of consciousness, or, as it has been called by esoteric scholars in the West, *cosmic consciousness*. This is why the kundalini

49

power is used in meditation. The art of meditation was presented in depth in volume two of this trilogy, *Religious Mysteries of the Orient*.

There is wisdom and knowledge expressed in the phrase of antiquity, "Be ye wise as the serpent."

In the next chapter, I will instruct you in Pranayamic methods of oriental rhythmic breathing which will stir the kundalini, and advance you up the road to mastery.

The balcony of the Udaipur Palace. The intiricate carvings depict Rajput princes in regal array amidst the delicately carved floral window panels presenting excellent examples of India's superlative art forms.

4

Oriental Rhythmic Breathing Techniques

In the Hindu practice of Pranayama, in which prana is generated, directed, and applied in various ways by certain methods of breathing, it will be found that the principle of *rhythm* is present in all these techniques. This is based upon the recognition by the Hindu Sages of the important part played by rhythm in the activities of the Universe.

Everything in the cosmos is in constant motion. The difference in things arises chiefly by reason of their varying rates of vibratory motion. All motion proceeds according to a definite rhythm or measured beat. As scientists express it, "Everything beats time—in measured rhythm."

A leading authority in physical science says, "Rhythm is a necessary characteristic of all motion. Given the coexistence everywhere of antagonistic forces—a postulate which is necessitated by our experience—rhythm is a necessary corollary. All motion alternates, be it the motion of planets in their orbits, or ethereal corpuscles in their undulations, be it in the cadence of speech, or the rise and fall of prices, it becomes manifest that this perpetual reversal of motion between limits is inevitable."

In nature, on all sides, in all phenomena, we find the evidence of the universality of rhythm. The atoms, the electrons, and the even smaller particles of matter which science has recently discovered manifest a regular circular swing. The planets swing in measured rotation around the sun. The tides rise and fall in regular movement. Day is followed by night, and night by day, in rhythmic measure. Summer and winter succeed each other in measured rhythm. Sleeping and waking states proceed in rhythmic sequence. Every pendulum swings backwards and forwards in measured time. Work and rest, in rhythmic beat, is manifested by all living things. Involution is followed by evolution, and evolution is succeeded by involution, in rhythmic order. All things physical, and all things mental, manifest their rising and falling tides. The pendulum of Nature is always swinging backwards and forwards, over and over again, according to the great law of universal rhythm.

The Hindu sages attach great importance to the maintenance of rhythm in the Pranayama breathing. They hold that in this way they "become in tune" with the rhythmic vibrations of Nature, and are thus able to partake of her energies and strength. They hold that by falling in with certain established rhythms of Nature, the magician is able to manifest power which otherwise would not be at his disposal. Accordingly, by mastering the inner rhythm of certain manifestations of prana, the magician is able to master, control, and direct the energies and forces of prana according to his desires and will. In the rhythmic beathing in Pranayama, the Yogis seek to establish a rhythmic motion of the prana, and thus awaken, arouse, and direct the action of the kundalini, or to direct the forces of prana in any course desired.

Yogi Ramacharaka, in his consideration of this phase of the subject, says, "The body one occupies is like a small inlet running into the land from the sea. Although apparently subject only to its own laws, it is really subject to the ebb and flow of the tides of the ocean. The great sea of life is swelling and receding, rising and falling, and we are responding to its vibrations and rhythms constantly. In a normal condition we receive the vibrations and rhythms of the great ocean of life, and respond to them. But at times the mouth of the inlet seems to be choked up with debris, and we fail to receive the impulse from Mother Ocean, and, as a consequence, inharmony manifests within us. You have heard how a note on a violin, if sounded repeatedly and in measured, regular rhythm, will start into motion certain vibrations which in time will destroy the bridge. The same result occurs when a regiment of soldiers cross a bridge, the order always being to "break step" on such an occasion, lest the vibration bring down both bridge and regiment.

"These manifestations of the effect of rhythmic motion will give you an idea of the effect on the body of rhythmic breathing. The whole system catches the vibration and becomes in harmony with the will, which causes the rhythmic motion of the lungs, and while in such complete harmony will respond readily to orders from the will. With the body thus attuned, the Yogi finds no difficulty in increasing the circulation in any part of his body by an order of the will, and, in the same way, he can direct an increased current of nerve force to any part or organ, strengthening and stimulating it. In like manner, the Yogi by rhythmic breathing 'catches the swing,' as it were, and is able to absorb and control a greatly increased amount of prana, which is then at the disposal of his will."

The Yoga teachings concerning rhythmic breathing hold that while the element of rhythmic breathing exercises is an all important feature of Pranayama, it is equally true that there can be no fixed and invariable rate of rhythm to be practiced alike by all persons. Rather, it is held that each person has his or her own individual rhythm that must be ascertained and then followed in the practice of Pranayama.

This individual rhythmic rate is discovered by learning the pulse beat rhythm of the individual. This, when learned, is to be regarded as the rhythmic measure of the person, and is to be adhered to in all his or her practice of rhythmic breathing.

The pulse beat of course, is due to the rhythmical expansions of the arteries caused by the repeated currents of blood sent through them by the beat of the heart. These rhythmical expansions are plainly discernible to anyone who places his finger upon an artery. There are several points on the body in which this may be detected. Simpliest, and most used, is the point on the thumb side of the wrist, which is employed by phsicians for "taking the'pulse" of the patient. At that point the artery is near the surface, and is readily pressed back against the wrist bone, making it easy to take the pulse.

The pulse beat varies considerably in a healthy person according to age, temperament, exercise or rest, emotional states, time of day, posture, atmospheric pressure, and personal idiosyncrasy. Before birth, the average number of pulsations each minute is 150; in the newly born, from 140 to 130; during the first year of life, 130 to 115; during the second year, 115 to 100; about the seventh year, 90 to 85; about the fourteenth year, 85 to 80; in adult life, 80 to 71; in old age, 70 to 60. In the female and in persons of a sanguine temperament, the pulse rate is more rapid by several beats per minute than in males and individuals of a phlegmatic type. The rate is also higher after a meal and during exercise, in the evening than in the morning, and in a standing than in a sitting or recumbent position. High temperatures also accelerate it. During sleep the pulse is usually slower than in the waking state. Forty is not an uncommon rate. In disease, the pulse presents wide variations in rate, regularity, and pressure.

The ancient Hindu teachings hold that in addition to the regular pulse beat of the body, that there is a special circulation in the brain which has a special rhythmic beat of its own. This special beat, it is claimed, does not throb in unison with the beating of the heart, but, instead is measured by the rate of breathing in the individual.

An American writer touches upon the subject, "While it is well covered in Eastern philosophies, it is little known in the occident—in fact, I have rarely spoken to a doctor who knew it, there is unquestionably a different rate of circulation within the brain than in the rest of the body. The pulse rate is the same all over the body, even in the covering of the brain, regulated by the heart beat, But the circulation of the brain itself is synchronous with not the heart pulsation, but the breathing rate: that is, twelve or fourteen beats to the minute. This is a very striking fact, and has been demonstrated by anatomical experiments made in England which certainly seem to bear out the Hindu contention that there is a definite connection between brain activity and the breathing rhythm."

The ancient teachings have even gone further in this direction, and explain that there is a positive relation between the pulse beats and the special "beat" in the circulation of the brain; that is to say, so many pulse beats to so many brain beats. By ascertaining this, they have been able to work out a system of rhythmic breathing in which just so many pulse beats are taken as the unit for certain inhalations and exhalations of the breath. The method is worked out precisely. Here follows the rules for Yoga Rhythmic Breathing. I suggest you study them first, before practicing any of the methods which will be presented. RULE ONE. Ascertain the rate of your normal pulse beat in this special manner:

Forget about time in relation to the pulse beat, as is customary; in other words, do not try to discover "how many beats to the minute," as physicians do. Instead, after acquiring a quiet state of mind and body place your fingers on your pulse, and then mentally count the beats, thus: one, two; one, two; one, two; etc., associating the pulse beats in your mind as one would the ticking of a clock. Catch the rhythm of the beats so they are impressed clearly upon your mind. Catch the time, as it were, just as you would in listening to music, the beating of a drum, the cadence of a marching parade, or the clickety-click of a passing train as its wheels strike the rails in regular time.

Having captured the "time" of the rhythmic pulse beats in your mind, begin to put them together in groups of six units, as you count one, two, three, four, five, six; one, two, three, four, five, six; etc. Practice this often, and you will soon find that you will instictively "catch the time." Your subconscious will soon take over the task for you, and you will become like a musician who is able to count time without conscious effort.

Once you have acquired proficiency in counting the time of the pulse beats and feeling their rhythm, you are ready to put into operation the next rule in the oriental breathing techniques.

RULE TWO. Employ the rate of your pulse beat as your unit of rhythmic breathing. Each beat counts as 1. When you are told to count to six, or 3, it means you are to count six or three pulse beats. When you are told to inhale six units, it means that you are to inhale your breath while counting six pulse beats of time. As you have learned how to automatically "catch the rhythm" of your pulse beats, you will soon be able to do this mentally without having to keep your finger on the pulse in the process.

RULE THREE. The time for each inhalation is always 6 units. The time for each exhalation is also always 6 units. Thus your inhalation and exhalation measure alike. The time for each retention of the breath is always 3 units. Accordingly, you will observe that retention measures only one half of inhalation or exhalation, and your exercise proceeds as follows: Inhale the breath for a count of 6 units; retain the breath for a count of 3 units; exhale the breath for a count of 6 units; then repeat this rhythmic breathing in like measure over and over. You may commit this measure to memory, as, 6-3-6; 6-3-6; 6-3-6; 6-3-6; etc.

RULE FOUR. Do not hurry through the Rhythmic Breathing Exercises. Take your time. Proceed leisurely. Never practice the exercises when you are hurried, or rushed.

RULE FIVE. Do not tire yourself in the exercises. The exercises are intended to rest you, not to tire you. Do not overdo the exercises. If you feel a slight dizziness, stop at once, for that session. The best results are often obtained with but a few moments of exercise at a time.

RULE SIX. Avoid anything like over straining or exertion in the exercises; they are designed to give you psychic strength, not to see how much air you can pump into your lungs. Never breathe in more air than is comfortable for your lungs to hold. Use moderation in the amount of air you inhale and in the time devoted to the exercise.

RULE SEVEN. Above all, do not try to retain the breath in the lungs beyond the measured time unit of three pulse beats. You are warned against prolonged holding-in of your breath; 3 units is exactly the right amount of time to retain it, and then exhale in the 6 unit rhythm.

Having learned the rules, you are prepared to proceed with the Oriental Rhythmic Breathing Exercises, always remembering the *6-3-6 count* of inhaling during the time of 6 units, retaining the breath during only 3 units, and, finally, exhaling the breath during 6 units. The culminated result is a rather slow breathing in and breathing out, with an ordinary pause for the holding in of breath, all tuned in timing to the rhythm of your pulse beats. The process will soon become automatic for you everytime you sit down to practice the exercise. At other times, it is not necessary to breathe rhythmically.

The Temple of Surya (The Sun God) at Konarak, on the Bay of Bengal. The entire temple was conceived as a horse-drawn chariot with twelve great wheels on either side. Courtesy Oxford Book and Stationary Company, Calcutta, India.

While crowds of natives watch, this Hindu Fakir sleeps upon a bed of thorns, showing absolute self-control.

This native magician of India sits for hours immobile in meditative contemplation.

ALTERNATE NOSTRIL BREATHING

In the Yoga teaching, emphasis is placed upon the importance of alternate nostril breathing; that is in the using of first one nostril, and then the other, in the act of breathing, one nostril being "shut off" by the pressure of the finger to its side while the other one performs its function. It is only when the oriental teaching concerning the two currents of pranic energy, the Ida and the Pingala, are understood that one begins to get an inkling of the reason for the practice of this method. Let us consider this principle for a few moments.

I have shown you in the preceding chapter that the pingala, or right hand channel of the sushumna, carries the *positive* currents of pranic energy, and the ida, or left hand channel, carries the *negative* currents.

The Yogis teach that if one is tired and feels a need of renewed energy, he may obtain the desired strength by breathing through the pingala (right hand) nostril, for a few moments, shutting off the left hand nostril by the pressure of the forefinger tip to the side of the nostril. In this way, one obtains the benefits of the positive currents alone.

On the other hand, if one feels nervous, worried or under tension, and feels the need of calmness, poise, confidence, and harmony, he may obtain the desired effect by breathing through the ida (left hand) nostril, holding the other nostril closed as previously mentioned. In this way he obtains the benefit of the negative currents alone.

Let me emphasize the value of this alternate breathing technique to you as it is a very useful method in times of stress to secure strength and energy, or poise and rest.

The Yogis also teach that nature provides for mental, physical, and emotional balance in the individual by an involuntary shifting of the breath from one nostril to the other, in alternate measure, depending upon the hour of the day or night. They claim that at certain hours of the daily twenty-four, a person is found to be breathing chiefly through one particular nostril, the use of other being comparatively slight. Later on, at a succeeding hour, the process is found to be reversed, and the other nostril is now the active one.

Now, the Hindu magicians claim to have discovered that there are certain occult advantages to be gained by a voluntary practice of alternate breathing. In this way a correlated rhythmic activity is established which is productive of an alternate play of action and reaction between the positive and negative pranic currents. This, once developed produces a state of mental, physical, and emotional harmony which is accompanied by a state of mental, physical, and emotional strength and power.

As Parimal Bandhu explained it, "By the process of alternate breathing, we can control the various nerve currents that are running through the body. First, we begin by recognizing them, and then we slowly get control of them. The Yogis consider that there are three main currents of prana in the human body. One they call Ida, another Pingala, and the third Sushumna. Pingala is on the right side of the spinal column, the Ida is on the left side, and in the middle of the spinal column is the Sushumna, a vacant channel. Pingala and Ida are the currents operating in every man and woman, and through these curreny we perform the functions of life. Sushumna is likewise present in every person, as a possibility, but is in operation only in the Yogi and those of high psychical development. The aim of the magician is to achieve the ability of putting the Sushumna into operation, and the means of achieving this aim is through the science of Pranayma via the control of the breath.

"The method of Oriental Rhythmic Breathing for putting the Sushumna into operation is this: let the student practice breathing in a harmonious, rhythmical manner for a few days, following which he may begin the practice of alternate breathing in a special way. The right nostril is closed off, and the lungs are slowly filled through the Ida, the left nostril, at the same time concentrating the mind and visualizing the passing of the nerve current down the Ida (the left side of the spinal column) and striking on the last plexus, which is the seat of the Kundalini. Hold the current there for a short time, and then visualize slowly drawing that nerve current with the breath through the triangular shaped plexus to the other side of the spinal column (the Pingala side). At this point, release the right nostril and close off the left, and slowly exhale the breath through the right nostril as the current is visualized as passing up the Pingala (the right side of the spinal column).

"The process is now performed in reverse. In other words, while still closing off the left nostril inhale slowly thru the right nostril while visualizing the nerve current as passing down the Pingala to strike upon the right side of the

last plexus, passing through the Kundalini from right to left this time. Then close off the right nostril and release the left, and as you exhale through the left nostril visualize the nerve current as ascending up the Ida.

"Thus the process is continued alternating back and forth the breathing and the visualizing of the nerve currents, and is repeated as desired. It functions as a means of charging the Kundalini with Prana, causing "the serpent power" to stir and eventually rise and ascend the vacant channel of the Sushumna. Admitedly the technique is not easy, but this is the alternate rhythmic breathing method as practiced by the magicians, which combined with the proper concentration developes power."

Aside from its magicial uses, alternate breathing renews the human battery, and electrifies all the nerve currents of the body. It stimulates organic functions to high activity, and brings well being and harmony to the individual. Here is a simple method of alternate breathing for this healthful purpose. Follow these seven points in the practice:

1   Assume a relaxed posture (asana).

2   Begin the exercise with a thorough breathing out (exhaling) of the air in your lungs using both nostrils.

3   Then, press your extended forefinger against the side of your right nostril, thus shutting off the inflow of air through it, and *inhale* deeply through your left nostril, counting 6 units during the inhalation.

4   Retain the breath in the lungs for 3 units.

5   Then press your finger against the side of your left nostril and release the right nostril, and *exhale* the breath slowly through it for 6 units.

6   Then while still maintaining pressure in shutting off the left nostril, inhale the breath slowly through the right nostril for 6 units.

7   Retain this breath in the lungs for 3 units. Then release the left nostril, close off the right, and exhale the breath slowly through the right nostril.

The process then begins all over, exhaling and inhaling through one nostril, and then the other, *alternately*, while always maintaing the count of 6 units in inhalation, 3 units in retention, and 6 units in exhalation.

Perform the exercise for only a few minutes at each session. Do not overdo it.

THE ASANAS

The Yogis lay great stress upon the subject of "asanas," which means the right postures or physical carriage when performing Pranayama and esoteric practices. The Yogi aphorism states, "The ideal of asana is relaxation, ease, and balance of mind and body."

In the study of Raja Yoga (physical Yoga), a series of physical and mental exercises are gone through everyday, until certain states are realized. Therefore, it is necessary that we find a posture in which we can remain in long periods in comfort. The rule is: the posture which is easiest for the particular person is the posture for that particular person to use.

Sculpture on the facade of the Hoysaleswara Temple, Halebid, India. Built following the death of King Kulottuga, A.D 1118, the temple stands to this day as the finest example in the world of Hoysalas of Dwarsamudra architecture and sculpture. Courtesy the Archaeological Survey of India.

During the practice of Pranayama, there is a good deal of action going on within the body. Nerve currents are displaced and given a new channel. New sorts of vibrations begin; the whole constitution is remodeled. The main part of this action lies along the spinal column, so that the one most important necessity for the correct asana is to hold the spinal column free by sitting erect, and holding the chest, neck, and head in a straight line.

Let the whole weight of the body be supported by the ribs, and then you will have an easy, natural posture, with the spine straight. The spinal cord is inside the vertebral column, thus if you sit crookedly you disturb this spinal cord. Anytime you sit improperly (out of plumb) and try to perform the oriental mystical practices, you are doing yourself an injury. The spinal cord must be kept straight; the three parts of the body—the chest, neck, and head—must always be held in one line. With a little practice the proper asana will soon become as natural to you as the act of breathing.

The chief elements in the Yogi posture or asana which you should employ in your Pranayama methods are:

1   Assume an upright position of the sitting body, with head, neck, and chest in as nearly a straight line as possible.

The historical Red Fort of Delhi, India. Built by the Moghul emperor, Shahjahan in 1649 in memorial of his empress at Agra. Behind the red sandstone walls are spacious lawns, palaces, and airy pavillions. Within one marble room of the fort, ceilinged in solid silver, is a couplet written in letters of gold which reads, "if there be a paradise on earth, 'tis here, it is here, it is here."

2   Throw your shoulders back, and do not permit your chest to sag inward.

3   Place your hands in your lap, palms upward, the back of one hand resting in the palm of the one beneath it, in an easy, comfortable position.

4   Have the weight of your body resting easily and evenly on the hips, thus being supported naturally.

5   Draw your abdomen slightly in, and never allow it to protrude.

This ancient Hindu formula for assuming what is called "the stable asana" may be useful to you. It was given by the venerable Sage, Yogi Patanjali of many centuries ago:

"Sitting erect, throw back your shoulders and hold your chest in the natural, outcurved position, letting your trunk rest its weight on your hips. Then let your body sway backward and forward a few inches in either direction, until you discover the exact point of the center of gravity of your body; you will know when this is found by the feeling of perfect balance and poise which will be experienced by you. This once found, you will have discovered the position in which you may sit for the longest time with the least feeling of fatigue or discomfort. There must be no bending forward, no craning forward of the neck, no protruding of the abdomen, no sagging of the chest. Neither must there be any leaning to one side or the other; your trunk must be supported by the spine and ribs, the weight resting evenly upon the two hips, and not upon one hip or the other. Neither must there be a sinking-down of the body, with the resulting 'sitting on the spine' which is neither a true sitting nor yet a true lying-down, but rather a mixture of both, and an unworthy position for a Yogi."

In the next chapter of this book, I shall instruct you further into specific techniques of Oriental Rhythmic Breathing for various purposes, and of the force and power of prana. As your studies advance, you will learn of the production and direction of prana in the various manifestations of the real magic of India. You will discover how the power of the ·mind is immeasurably increased when pranic energy is added to it, and this pranic energy is aroused and made available by means of the practice of Pranayama.

5

Yogi Pranayama Practices

By means of arousing into activity the power of prana, the Yogis are able to direct the pranic energy, by the use of the will, into the various parts and organs of their bodies, thus strengthening them to a great degree. By similar methods, they are able to revitalize others and perform various forms of mental healing which is regarded as one of the magics of India.

Also the pranic energy is used in various of psychic phenomena, such as telepathy, mental influence, etc. The Masters teach that all students of the magical power should add to their knowledge all methods of the arousing and projection of pranic force, in which the practice of "rhythmic beathing" plays an important part. I will now give you the very essence of this instruction.

NADI BREATHING EXERCISES

The Nadis are psychic nerve channels which extend to all parts of the body in countless number, and which serve to carry the prana to every organ and part thereof. The Yogi teach that these channels of the nadis must be kept open and free, so as to allow an uninterrupted flow of prana through them. They have designed special exercises for this purpose. There are specifically three of these: "The Nadi Purifier," "The Nadi Stimulator," and "The Nadi Vibrator."

The Nadi Purifying Exercise should be used at the beginning of any practice of rhythmic breathing as it clears and cleanses, purifies and rends free the channels of the nadis, and thus allows for an excellent flow of prana through the system. It is performed by this fourfold process:

1   Assume the stable and easy Asana.

2   Inhale a deep breath, using both nostrils during the count of 6 units.

3   Retain the breath for 3 units.

4   Shape your lips as if you intended to whistle, and then silently whistle out the breath through your pursed lips, using considerable vigor and propelling force in doing so. Perform this special method of exhaling the breath during the count of 6 units.

Repeat the process seven times without haste or overexertion. Then rest a few minutes before undertaking any other breathing exercise.

In addition to its employment as a preliminary to further rhythmic breathing, this Nadi Purifier Exercise will be found very helpful when you are tired or fatigued in any way; in which case, it will be well to continue it with The Nadi Stimulator Exercise which follows.

This exercise should be used at the conclusion of any practice of rhythmic breathing as it stimulates the nadis, and accordingly stimulates the entire nervous system, and the body in general. Like the previous nadis exercise, it is accomplished through a fourfold process:

1 Stand erect, with head, neck, and back held straight, shoulders thrown back, abdomen slightly drawn in, and legs straight and stiff.

2 Inhale fully for 6 units.

3 Retain the breath for 3 units as you perform this "muscle movement:" extend both arms straight out in front of you, on a line with the shoulders, fists clenched—not stiffly, but in an easy straight position; slowly draw your clenched fists back to your shoulders, contracting the arm muscles as you do so, so that when the fists reach the shoulders the arms will be stiff and taut. At this point in the exercise . . .

4 Exhale the breath for 6 units.

Repeat the exercise seven times in a leisurely manner, then rest for a few moments. A little practice is necessary in order to acquire the knack of the peculiar "snap" of the muscle movements. The exercise has a bracing, tonic effect.

The Nadi Vibrator Exercise is employed when you feel an apathetic condition of mind and body. The exercise tends to "shake up" the whole system, and its vibrating influence removes stagnation from the circulatory and nervous systems. It is performed as follows:

1 Assume the stable and easy Asana.

2 Inhale during the count of 6 units, but instead of drawing the breath in the regular manner as a steady, continuous inhalation, inhale in a series of short, vigorous sniffs, just as if you were sniffing at a pungent substance.

3 Retain the breath for 3 units.

4 Exhale the breath in a long, deliberate restful "sighing" breath, for a count of 6 units.

Repeat this exercise seven times; then rest for a few minutes. The peculiar "vibrating effect" of this exercise will suggest its employment at times when you feel sluggish.

MANTRAM VOCAL CULTIVATION

A mantram is a religio/magical recitation used by the Hindus. It is repeated over and over in rhythm. The Yogis place great emphasis on the beauty of the voice and cadance in such performances.

Swami Vivekananda has this to say on the matter, "By right practice a beautiful voice will come to you. The Yogis are noted for their wonderful voices, which are strong, smooth, and clear, and have wonderful trumpet-like carrying power."

This impressive archway overlooking the harbor in Bombay is known as "The Gateway to Western India." From here one can travel to explore the far corners of India in the search for her magic.

An illuminated front view of the Maharaja's Palace at Mysore. Seen at night in glowing splendor it forms a never-to-be-forgotten memory of Oriental beauty.

Among the numerous breathing exercises employed by the Yogis for developing the desired quality of voice, the most famous is known as The Mantram Pathfinder. This exercise is practiced as follows:

1 Assume the stable and easy Asana.
2 Inhale as usual for 6 units.
3 Retain the breath for three units.
4 Opening the mouth as in singing, exhale through the opened mouth for the usual 6 units, at the same time sounding the notes described below.
5 Repeat the exercise seven times, avoiding haste and overtiring your voice. Then rest for a few minutes before practicing futher.

The sounds or notes used during the exercise consist of seven droning or humming sounds produced with the exhaled breath; one sound for each exhalation. The drone or hum produced is like a whirring sound, and the concluding humming sound of "m-m-m-m-m-m-m" must always be quite marked and persistent. The vowel sound of the *hummmmmmm* is varied with each of the seven repetitions of the exercise, as follows:

1 Sound "Hah" followed by the "m-m-m-m-m" hum so as to sound like "Hahm-m-m-m-m-m-m-m."
2 In the same way sound "Haw" followed by the hum, as "Hawm-m-m-m-m-m-m."
3 In the same way sound "Hee" followed by the hum, as "Heem-m-m-m-m-m-m."
4 In the same way sound "High" followed by the hum, as "Highm-m-m-m-m-m-m."
5 In the same way sound "Hoe" followed by the hum, as "Hoem-m-m-m-m-m-m."
6 In the same way sound "Hoo" followed by the hum, as "Hoom-m-m-m-m-m-m."
7 In the same way sound "Hum" followed by the "m-m-m-m-m-m-m-m-m," thus making the full sound of "Hum-m-m-m-m-m-m-m-m-m."

The droning or humming sound of "m-m-m-m-m-m-m-m" will easily follow the vowel sound in each instance when you close your lips after making the latter, and continue the hummmmmmm with closed lips. With practice, "The Mantram Pathfinder" will bring you a beautiful voice.

Yogi Ramackaraka suggests another vocal exercise used by the Hindus which will cultivate an outstanding voice. You can use this exercise in combination with the foregoing, if you wish. The exercise consists of puckering up the mouth as if you were about to whistle through it (or to say "Whew") and then, while holding that position of the lips and face, sing naturally through the puckered lips, sounding the notes through them without distrubing the position of the lips. Practice this exercise a little each day, and note how your speaking voice improves.

THE GRAND YOGA BREATH

This a popular form of pranic breathing in India . The Yogis practice it in order to call into activity the whole nervous system and centers of the body, and to distribute the prana to the plexuses which serves as its natural reservoirs and "storage batteries of prana." In "The Grand Yoga Breath Exercise" the various chakras are aroused to activity, and, at the same time, the nadis are stimulated and energized. In it, also, the power of creative mind is invoked and applied in an effective manner. The exercise is performed as follows:

(A) Lie down flat on your back, keeping the head, neck, back, and legs in a straight line. The position must be easy and natural.

(B) Perform the usual cycles of rhythmic breathing as you have learned, i.e., inhalation for 6 units, retention for 3 units, exhalation for 6 units. Perform these cycles of rhythmic breathing for seven times, with a few moments of rest between each cycle. Now accompany each inhalation, in turn, with one of the following mental exercises, in the order given, the first with the first cycle, the second with the second cycle, and so on until the seven have been performed, one with each cycle, viz.:

1   Visualize the breath as entering the body through the bones of the legs and then exhaled through them. Try to "feel" as strongly as possible that this action is really occurring.

2   Visualize the breath as entering the body through the bones of the arms, and then exhaled through them, accompanying this with the "feeling," as above instructed.

3   Visualize the breath as entering the body through the top of the skull, and then exhaled through it; accompanying this with the appropriate "feeling."

4   Visualize the breath as entering the body through the stomach, and then exhale through it; accompanying this with the appropriate "feeling."

5   Visualize the breath as entering the body through the reproductive organism, and then exhaled through it; accompanying this with the appropriate "feeling."

6   Visualize the breath as entering the body through the base of the spinal column, and then exhaled through it; accompanying this with the appropriate "feeling."

7   Visualize the breath as entering the body through every pore of the skin all over the whole body, from head to foot; accompanying this with the appropriate "feeling."

Having rested for a few moments following this first stage of "The Grand Yoga Breath Exercise," you are now ready to perform the second stage of the exercise, which is as follows:

(A) Lie on the back in the same position, and with the same care, as in the first stage of the exercise.

(B) Perform seven more cycles of rhythmic breathing, following the same rhythm, i.e., Inhalation 6 units; retention 3 units; exhalation 6 units. During each inhalation perform the visualization (and accompanying "feeling") of sending the pranic current to each of the chakras, in turn, one with each exhalation, in the order named. At the same time, use the will to "*will*" that the current will go where it is directed (where it is visualized as going and is "felt" as going).

By this procedure, each chakra is energized and stimulated by the inflowing prana thus directed to it. Here is the list of chakras to be reached in the way just instructed, in the order in which they are to be aroused in the exercise:

66

On stage with India's great illusionist, K. Lall and his company of magical entertainers. (Courtesy the Benjamin Kleinman Collection)

1 "The Muldahara Chakra," situated at the base of the spinal column.

2 "The Svadisthana Chakra," situated at the base of the reproductive organism.

3 "The Manipura Chakra," situated in the center of the trunk, just back of the Solar Plexus.

4 "The Anahata Chakra," situated in the region of the heart.

5 "The Visuddha Chakra," situated in the region of the throat.

6 "The Ajna Chakra," situated in the brain, just back of the center of the eyebrows.

7 "The Sahasraha Chakra," situated on the top of the head, at its center.

(C) "The Grand Yoga Breath Exercise" should be concluded by "visualizing," "feeling," and "willing" a great current of prana to sweep over the entire body, reaching every outer and inner part, bathing every organ, center and region with a great flow of pranic power and energy, and thus *vitalizing* the whole physical system, in its entirety.

THE LIVING BATTERY OF PRANA

The real East Indian magicians in producing their mysteries, require the employment of prana in connection with the creative mind, feel the necessity of regarding their body as "a living battery of prana," and keeping that battery well charged. To this end, they perform the following pranic exercise:

1   Assume the stable and easy Asana, with the following variation, i.e, place your feet close together, side by side, so as to close the circuit at that end. Also close the circuit at the other extreme of the limbs (the arms) by "locking the fingers of each hand in the following manner, viz., by placing the palm of one hand over and facing the other palm, the tips of the fingers of each hand resting hooked into the closed fingers of the other hand; the thumb of each hand touching the outer edge of the opposite hand just below the little finger on each. The position of the hands is simple to achieve once you try it.

2   Retaining this position, practice rhythmic breathing in the regular cycles, i.e., inhalation 6 units, retension 3 units, exhalation 6 units. Make your rhythmic breathing easily and naturally without effort.

3   While performing this rhythmic breath, "visualize," "feel," and "will" that the prana you are absorbing with each breath will be distributed in your closed circuit of "the living battery" in your body, as well as by all the pranic centers, chakras, and nadis.

The oriental magicians frequently sit in this attitude for sizable periods of time thus charging themselves with pranic energy in this closed-circuit exercise. They also employ these general principles for controlling emotions, removing unwanted ones and establishing desired ones. The method for this consists simply of practicing the rhythmic breathing exercise, with its proper Asana and characteristic "6-3-6" units of rhythm, during which process the magician "visualizes," "feels" and "wills" himself to experience the opposite emotion to that which he desires to master.

For example, if it is the emotion of fear or dread that one wishes to overcome, then the emotion of courage is visualized to supplant it. All undesirable emotions are negative in character, and the way to kill out negative is to concentrate upon the opposing positive, which, when used in conjunction with the pranic rhythmic breathing, has a powerful effect in such regard. You can use the method exactly as the magicians do to master your own emotions.

IMPARTING PRANIC ENERGY TO OTHERS

The skilled magician is not only able to charge himself with pranic energy, but, as desired, is able to charge other persons with the power as well. The following two methods are effective in this regard, the first of these is as follows:

1   Have the other person seated before you with toes touching yours, and hands clasped in yours.

2   Both yourself and the party to whom you are imparting pranic energy must practice rhythmic breathing in harmonious unison, observing the same rhythmic unit and "breathing in time with each other;" you setting the time measure according to your own pulse beat.

3   During the performance of the rhythmic breathing in unison, you must "visualize," "feel," and "will" the flow of prana as passing from out of yourself and into the other person—picturing, feeling, and willing it to flow through your hands into his or hers.

The second method for this purpose is to have the other person seated back to back with you; the two spinal columns touching each other, each person assuming the Asana position as used in "the living battery" process which you have studied. Then breathe "in unison," precisely as described in the first method while projecting the prana into the other person by "visualization," "feeling," and "willing" it to flow from one spinal column to the other.

Either of these two methods of imparting pranic energy to others may be used, and are employed by the magicians in helping the other person use these psychic methods to gain physical improvement, circumstances, etc. In all such cases (which the magicians refer to as "treatments by prana"), the thought of the desired improved condition is projected along with the flow of prana, by "visualizing," "feeling," and "willing!"

PRANAZING WATER

The magicians also practice a technique of charging water with prana, the water in turn being drunk by persons in need of a higher charging of prana within themselves. The method is particularly used in the treatment of ill persons.

In this Yogi practice, the glass or cup of water is held in the left hand, letting the bottom of same rest in the hollowed palm of that hand. Rhythmic breathing is then performed as has been instructed. The right hand is then held over the glass or cup in the process of this breathing; gather the fingertips together over the water, then shake them gently toward the water as if one were trying to throw from the fingertips little drops of water that had gathered on them. After a few moments of this "shaking," open the right hand and pass the palm slowly around the top of the glass or cup, about six inches above it. Perform this pass above the glass in a circular motion seven times. Through all of this process of pranazing the water, "visualize," "feel," and "will" the flow of prana into the water.

The Hindu magicians state that when pranazied water is drunk by the individual in need of it, such will aid in charging the person with the needful prana.

While we are dealing with the subject of prana healing methods, I will give you a more careful coverage of this form of real magic practiced in India. Yogi methods of psychic healing is applied in three general ways, viz., (1) by the use of the eye; (2) by the use of the breath; (3) by the use of the hands.

HEALING BY THE EYE

In the pranic treatment by the use of the eye, the Yogi healer practices rhythmic breathing, while at the same time, gazing fixedly into the eyes of the patient, and "visualizing," "feeling," and "willing" that a powerful flow of pranic energy will pour into the body of the patient, reaching the affected parts and restoring them to normal functioning; accompanying this projection is the thought and "mental picture" of the organ in question being normal in every respect.

HEALING BY THE BREATH

In the pranic treatment by the use of the breath, the Yogi healer practices rhythmic breathing, and in his exhalations he breathes directly upon the affected and ailing parts, or upon the surface of the skin directly above such. In some cases, the healer exhales his rhythmic breath upon a piece of flannel or cloth which is then placed over or upon the affected and ailing region of the body. This method produces a sensation of warmth and a general soothing effect upon the patient. During the process the healer constantly "visualizes," "feels," and "wills" the flow of prana, together with the desired result.

Healing by "the pranic breath" is a very old form of healing. It was practiced in India for thousands of years. In certain temples in India, the priests cure diseases by this method of breathing upon the patients; and thousands of cases are carried to the temples each year, often from points hundreds of miles distant. As I have mentioned, psychic healing is one of the magics of India.

HEALING BY THE HANDS

Pranic healing by the use of the hands is unquestionably the most commonly found form of healing of this kind, both in India and other lands. It is known in many countries as "the laying on of hands." Chapter four of the second volume of this trilogy, *Religious Mysteries of the Orient* is devoted to this subject.

In many cases, the treatment merely consists of "laying on the hands," accompanied by rhythmic breathing and appropriate visualization, etc., but there are several other forms of applying and directing the pranic force which I will now describe. In all of them the rhythmic breathing accompanies the use of the hands, combined with the "visualization," "feeling," and "willing" mental processes which the East Indian magicians say are absolutely essential to the success of the psychic treatments.

In general, making healing passes with the hands are used in this method of healing for the distribution of prana. One method is to extend the open fingers of each hand, like the sticks of a folding fan. Hold the opened hands about one foot from the body of the patient. Then raise them above the patient's head, and bring them down along the body in a slow, sweeping motion from his head to his feet. When the pass is completed, move the hands side wise, making a motion as though you were "flicking" water from them. Then close the fingers together,

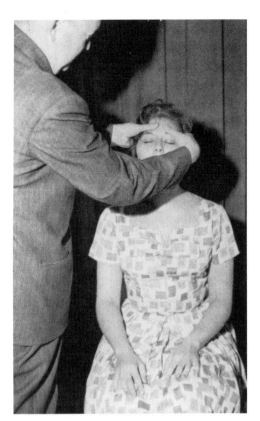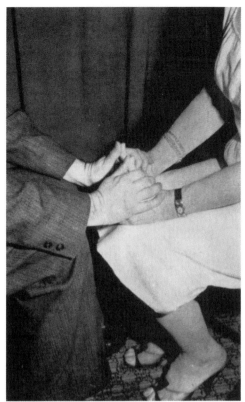

Showing various methods of projecting prana to the patient by the hands. In the upper photograph, the patient's hands are gripped by the magician, with the inside of the balls of thumbs touching. The prana is projected from thumbs to thumbs, and accordingly into the hands and up the arms. In the lower photograph, the prana is projected from the magician's hands encircling the patient's head; the thumbs are placed on the patient's forehead directly over the pineal gland.

and bring the hands up in a swinging movement along the sides of the patient's body until they extend above his head. Then repeat the passes, and so on until you feel that the treatment has been continued long enough, and the patient is sufficiently charged with healing prana.

All downward movements of the extended hands are soothing; all upward movements of the extended hands are invigorating. Sidewise passes of the extended hands have a "stirring up" or "loosening up" effect which is helpful in cases of congestion, etc.

Sometimes a rotary pass is found stimulating and helpful; the hands being rotated in front of the body of the patient, in the direction of moving the hands of a clock. Sometimes a "boring movement" of the extended forefinger is employed to increase the flow of blood to an area in need of cleansing. Letting the palms rest on the affected surface for a time also produces a healing effect; many Yogi healers employ this method almost exclusively. Others gently stroke the body with the extended fingers; the stroking always being in an outward and downward direction. Another variation form is "the vibration method," in which

Bathing in the Holy Ganges.

Looking out from a balcony of the Great Eastern Hotel towards the world famous Jain Temple. (From the Ron Ormond Collection)

the fingers are placed firmly over the affected part, and a vibrating movement then manifested by the hands.

In India, a Yogi will frequently "pranaize a handkerchief," using the same method as was given for pranaizing a glass of water; the charged handkerchief or cloth is then worn by the patient over the affected part.

The Yoga teaching holds that all forms of mental or psychic healing of all kinds, no matter under what name applied, are in reality accomplished by this same method via the projection of thought and will accompanied by prana. Swami Vivekananda has this to say on the subject: "We see sects in every country who have attempted the control of prana. In many countries of the world I have heard of this power being used under many different names, such as oydic force, animal magnetism, faith healing, etc., but if we analyze the different processes we shall find that the background of each is this control of prana, whether they know it or not. If you boil down their theories, the residuum will be the same. It is all the one and the same force they are using, only unknowingly. They have stumbled on the discovery of a force, and do not know its nature, but they are unconsciously using the same powers which the Yogi uses, and which comes from prana. All manifestations of power arise from this control. Many men do not know of this secret of the Yogis which is one of the most ancient of all, but this is the true explanation. These are among the various functions of Pranayama."

Prana is by no means only used in healing. It is the energy source of the manifestation of all forms of mental magic. Remember always this law of the great magicians, Thought, Will, and Prana constitute "The Threefold Powers"

72

of all magic, and the knowledge of this triple-key will enable you to open all of the many doors to mental mastery, magic and occult power.

As a student of the real magic of India, you have now learned of The Power Of Prana and how to develop it to energize your body by Yoga practices. It is your source of power. It is the energy behind magic. You will next learn specific details as to how the magician directs this energy through mastery of the mind.

The magnificent temple of Jainism, Calcutta, India.

6
The Mastery of the Mind

You will now learn of the controlling and the mastering of the mind in the processes of what the Yogis call Yama, or self-control, Dharana, or control of the thought processes, and Dhyana, or concentrated meditation.

In order to understand the Eastern teaching concerning Dharana and Dhyana, it is necessary that you become acquainted with the ancient knowledge concerning Chitta, or "mind stuff." Only then will you truly be able to understand the Hindu methods of the mastery of the mind.

It is held that chitta is a "substance" just as the akasha is a "substance." The latter is a tenuous physical substance, while the former is a mental substance. Both are regarded as being omnipresent, and wherever there is material substance there also will be found mental substance, so say the Masters. Likewise, state these teachers, both substances are capable of taking on innumerable forms, and assuming manifold appearances and combinations.

The chitta or "mind substance" is held as a universal principle by the magicians. Here is what two Masters have to say about it:

Yogi Ramacharaka says, "Chitta is a refined and subtle principle, rather than a substance akin to matter. But chitta is a 'substance' in the sense of 'that which underlies or stands under'—for it is the underlying substance of mind. Chitta may be considered as a higher phase of energy, for it bears the same relation to energy that energy bears to matter. Matter is the thing that the soul uses to clothe itself in, energy is the thing that the soul uses in order to act, and chitta is the thing the soul uses in order to think. Chitta is to mind what the akasha is to matter, or what energy is to force. Thought is a motion in chitta, just as matter is a motion in akasha—both manifest themselves in vortex form or whirlpools. Vritti, or 'waves of vibrations of thought,' are these whirlpools in and of chitta."

Swami Vivekananda says, "Chitta is the mind-stuff, and the vrittis are the waves and ripples rising in it when external causes impinge on it. All thought is but various processes in the mind-stuff called chitta. The waves of thought in the chitta are called vrittis (meaning literally 'the whirlpools'). What is thought?

74

Thought is a force, as is gravitation and repulsion. It is absorbed from the infinite store house of force in Nature. The instrument called chitta takes hold of that force, and when it passes out at the other end it is called *thought*.

"Memory and dreams are classes of vrittis. You hear a word; that word is like a stone thrown into the lake of chitta. It causes a ripple, and that ripple rouses a series of ripples; this is memory. When the peculiar kind of ripple called sleep throws the chitta into a ripple of memory, it is called a dream. Dream is another form of the ripple which in the waking state is called memory. The bottom of that lake is the true self; the lake is the chitta, and the waves are the vrittis. The bottom of the lake we cannot see, because its surface is covered with ripples. It is only when the ripples have subsided, and the water is calm, that we can catch a glimpse at the bottom. If the water is muddy, the bottom will not be seen; if the water is agitated all the time, the bottom will not be seen. If the water is clear, and there are no waves, we shall see the bottom. In this calmness we will see our true self; we will see our soul."

Patanjali, the ancient founder of Yoga, who lived about 300 B.C. and established the Hindu Yoga Philosophy has millions of followers in India and other lands. He devotes great attention to the subject of chitta and the vrittis. In fact, his "Yogi Aphorisms," the basis of his teachings, are made principally of references to chitta and directions for regulating the vrittis. His very first aphorism stated, "Now is the exposition of yoga to be made. Yoga is the regulation of the fluctuations of chitta."

According to the teachings of the magicians, attached to each particle of matter there is a little particle of mind—in much the same way that the fog out of doors is caused by a little moisture to attach itself to each of the dust particles in the air. In the same way, one might say, a little particle of "mind stuff" is attached to every atom in the Universe, so that every atom has its own particular "atom consciousness," as it were. When these atoms are bound together in the form, for example, as that of a starfish, then you will have the starfish consciousness. Or, if bound together in the form of a bird, then you will have the bird consciousness. Or, if bound together in the form of a man or woman, then you will have a man or woman consciousness.

When an object is presented to the mind and perceived, the latter is formed into the shape of the object perceived. It is held that these particles of "mind stuff" are agglomerated, thus forming the different units of consciousness. It is also held that concentration consists in getting more of these particles into one place. If you can condense them at a point, then you will have absolute unity of consciousness at that point, because you have concentrated the material of the "mind stuff" in a manner just as a magnifying glass will focus the sun's rays at a point. Thus "the mind stuff" is bound together at this point of concentration, and you have absolute concentration. It is then that The Creative Mind may go strongly into effect and matter may be created directly by mind.

DHARANA AND DHYANA

Having made you familiar with the Yogis' teachings concerning chitta and the vrittis, I shall now lead you along the path of Dharana (mental control) and

Dhyana (concentrated meditation). Also, I will include features of a third Hindu classification of mental phenomena, that of Pratyahara, or the control of the senses. From a practical point of view, the control of the senses, control of the mind, and concentrated meditation are so closely interrelated that I will group them together in one study.

Before proceeding further in this chapter dealing with the mastery of the mind, please understand that I am not teaching you these Hindu theories simply to present a lot of Yogi technicalities; I am teaching you these principles of oriental wisdom as they are the foundations upon which the actual structure, practices, and methods of the real magic of India are based.

Let us now study the Yoga teachings regarding the mental control known as Pratyahara (controlling of the senses) which is regarded as a preparatory stage of Dharma, or the control of the mind in general. Our senses furnish "the raw materials of thought," and it follows that control of sensations is the first step of complete mental control. In Pratyahara, the senses are mastered by the will, and the mind is thus made free for concentrated meditation (Dhyana) upon some chosen subject or object. Before the mind can obtain the "quiet power" enabling it to perform properly the processes of concentration and visualization, its senses must be so controlled that outside influences are shut out temporarily by the methods of Pratyahara.

The control of the senses in Pratyahara is accomplished by the exercise of attention; attention being distinctly an action of the will. The process is not one of the will holding a sensation in mind, but rather of holding a sensation out of mind. In other words, of keeping the sensation from entering consciousness. Western people are not strangers to this principle, as any person knows that they must give attention and cut out disturbing stimuli if they are going to concentrate. Psychologists explain that the more attention we give to a sensation the more we are aware of it. Conversely, the intensity of a sensation the more we are aware of it. Conversely, the intensity of a sensation may be decreased to its lowest point; even to the point of completely abolishing it. In this statement we have the essence of the Yoga teaching of Pratyahara. The Yogis have mastered this ability of blocking out sensations to an amazing degree, and are thus able to devote absolute thought to the object of their meditation. By the same process, they are able to "shut out" the most intense pain, simply by turning the attention away from it.

Swami Vivekananda in speaking of Pratyahara says, "All actions, internal and external, occur when the mind joins itself to certain centers. Willingly or unwillingly the mind is drawn to join itself to the centers, and they feel disturbance and sometimes even misery as a result. If the mind were under control such would not occur.

"What would be the result of controlling the mind? It then would not join itself to the centers of sensations and perceptions, and feeling and willing would be under control. It is perfectly possible to do this. The Yogis do this in their practice of Pratyahara, which means 'gathering together,' checking the outgoing powers of the mind, and free it from the thraldom of the senses. It is a positive process which is mastered through practice."

The Yogis' method of achieving Pratyahara is twofold, viz., (1) concentrating upon some object of importance and interest, while throwing intense and

Animals hold an esteemed place in Hindu philosophy. They are treated with great kindness all over India.

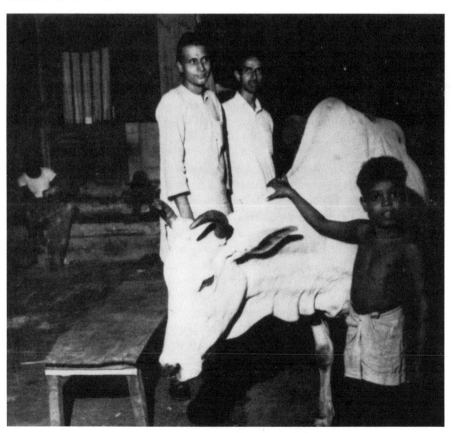

continuous attention into the task; and (2) refusing to allow the attention to "take hold of" or to "go out toward" any outside sight, sound, smell, taste, or touch. As you now learn of Dharana and Dhyana and study their mastery, you will, at one and the same time, be learning Pratyahara.

The Monument to Swami Vivekananda, whose teachings are so closely allied to the real magic of India. It is located on the southernmost tip of India where three oceans meet, and is regarded as a highly sacred spot.

DHARANA, OR CONTROL OF THOUGHT

In this important phase of Yoga teaching, in mastering the mind, there is sought (1) the positive control of the attention and its direction toward any selected subject or object; and (2) the control of the attention in the direction of preventing its "going out" towards outside sensations which seek to interfere with concentration.

In Dharana, the attention is intensely active in the work of "holding in consciousness" the desired subject or idea, and also in the work of "holding out of consciousness" all nonessentials not related to the matter being concentrated upon. In this we have the essence of complete concentration.

As Sadhu Parimal Bandu explained it, "Dharana is holding the mind to certain points; this means forcing the mind to be conscious of certain things to the exclusion of others. When the chitta, or 'mind stuff' is limited and confined to a certain point, this is called Dharana.

"How difficult it is to control the mind. Well has the mind been compared, in this Hindu story, to a maddened monkey:

'Once there was a monkey, restless by its own nature, as all monkeys are. As if that were not enough, someone made the monkey drink freely of wine, so that he became still more restless. Then a scorpion stung him; it made him jump about for a whole day. The poor monkey's condition became worse than ever. To complete his misery, a demon entered into him. What language can describe the uncontrollable restlessness of that monkey?'

78

"The human mind is like that monkey; incessantly active by its own nature. Then it becomes drunk by the wine of desire, thus increasing its turbulence. After desire takes possession, there comes the sting of the scorpion of jealousy of others whose desires meet with greater fulfillment. Last of all, the demon of pride takes possession of the mind, making it think itself of all importance. How hard it is to control such a mind. Yet, it is the task of Dharana to control that restless, drunk, scorpion bitten, demon possessed mind, and to make it do certain things, attend to certain things, while refraining from doing other things and attending to distracting things. It is hard, but it can be done. The Yogis do it. The successful magicians do it, and you, too, must learn the mastery of your mind, if you would practice the real magic."

In achieving Dharana, you must achieve the ability of expelling unwanted thoughts at will. It is well worth the practice required, for then instead of being ruled by unwanted ideas, we eliminate them and concentrate only upon those we desire. If you can expel and inhibit a thought—practically killing it dead for the time being, as it were—you can do anything else with it that you please. This is an ability of great value as it not only frees a man from mental torment, but it gives him a concentrated power of handling mental work absolutely unknown to him before. It is thus the object of Yoga, through the practice of Dharana, to enable the mind to do away with all the thoughts which you do not want, to pick out and choose those you do want, and ultimately to pinpoint the one thought which is to become the entire center of your concentration.

DHYANA, OR CONCENTRATED MEDITATION

Dhyana, or concentrated meditation, is closely allied to both Dharana, or control of the thoughts, and Pratyahara, or control of the senses. In the next chapter of this book, I will instruct you in the practical methods of oriental concentration that embraces all three of these related phases of mind. First, though, I will give you some of the more mystical aspects of Dhyana, as taught by the Yogis, as it will deepen your understanding of oriental wisdom.

There are two phases of Yogi Dhyana, viz., (1) concentrated meditation upon some definite, concrete subject or object—this is called "Concrete Dhyana;" and (2) concentrated meditation upon some indefinite, abstract subject or object, perhaps even upon some transcendental matter—this is called "Abstract Dhyana."

Concrete Dhyana is closely linked to Dharana, or control of the thoughts. Abstract Dhyana, on the other hand, is closely linked to Samadhi, or mystic contemplation. Concrete Dhyana is practical and usable in connection with controlling and mastering the mind. Abstract Dhyana is metaphysical and semireligious.

In Abstract Dhyana, a person enters into a state of concentration. It is not concentration upon concrete physical or mental things, rather it is concentration upon the transcendental and the abstract; things in themselves being considered apart from their forms and manifestations. There is a search for the inner knowledge, the inner nature of things, as apart from sense knowledge— the nature of things which would persists if there were no mental faculties to perceive them, and no mind to know them. In this we have meditation.

Swami Vivekananda speaks of meditation this way, "The meditative state is the highest state of existence. So long as there is desire, no real happiness can come. It is only the contemplative study of things that brings us real enjoyment and happiness. The animal has happiness in the senses; the man has happiness in the intellect; the gods have happiness in spiritual contemplation. It is only to the soul that has attained to this contemplative state that the world really becomes beautiful. To him who desires nothing, and does not mix himself up with them, the manifold changes of nature are one panorama of beauty and sublimity. These ideas have to be understood in the Dhyana of meditation. When the power of Dhyana has become so much intensified as to be able to reject the external part of perception, and remain meditating only on the internal part and the meaning thereof, that state is called Samadhi."

Abstract Dhyana belongs to the mystics, Concrete Dhyana belongs to the magician. We shall direct our attention towards the latter as we learn now of the power of concentration.

Within the first Cave of Ajanta is seen this gigantic figure of Lord Buddha depicted in meditation. The door panels to the sacred room are designed with floral patterns and in front are seen the two "Dwawapalas" or doorkeepers. The Ajanta Caves are thirty-four in number and were carved from solid rocks between the fourth and ninth centuries A.D.

7

The Power of
Concentration

The East Indian magicians are keenly aware of the wonderful power of the human mind when it is mastered, developed, and manifested in the process of concentration. They have devised methods of applying that power most effectively. In fact, the word "concentration" fully expresses the fundamental working principle of oriental magic and psychic powers.

The Hindu teaching is that only by and through concentration are possible the manifestations of the Creative Mind Principle—the creation of the mental image (or ideal) being so clearly and powerfully held that the materialization thereof follows in an efficient manner and degree. The teaching is that mind-power, like any other kind of power, manifests intensively only when its field is narrowed and its energies are focused to a fine point in concentration.

The magicians in their supernormal control of Nature, have mastered the science of concentration. They have done this through the careful study of Yoga, and by diligent practice have put into effect the methods of Pratyahara, Dharana, and Dhyana achieving mastery of the mind. They have also acquired the art of perfect concentration in mastering its two cardinal principles, viz., (1) the focusing or bringing to "one pointedness" the attention, and holding this upon the desired objective; and (2) the inhibiting or "shutting out" of all outside distractions that would in any way interfere with their complete concentration. Such is the mastery of the magician.

The magician has also acquired the equally important skill of being able to close the doors of attention and thought upon any subject or object, after he has completed his concentrated consideration thereof. Thus, he keeps his mind free and unhampered at all times, so that he may give his full and undivided attention to each new thing that demands the use of his mind. The magician's attention is like a great searchlight which is applied with intense power to any object upon which it is turned, but which is easily turned away from that object when the purpose of the application of its light has been accomplished. In other words, the magician is able to detach his mind from any and all subjects at will—thus giving the mind relaxation and rest when such are needed, building mental strength.

There is a lesson here from the East to the West, as many great occidental scholars are able to think, but are not able "not to think" at will. Both of these positive and negative aspects of thought are of equal importance, and both are achieved by the magician.

I will now give you specific instruction in developing the power of your concentration in the exact manner of the East Indian magician. In this instruction, consider the basic principle as the main thing, allowing the details to be secondary, as such may possibly be varied to suit your own particular accomplishments. There is much food for thought in this phase of the instruction, and if it is your desire to learn of the presentation of the real magic of India, I suggest that you devote care, time, and attention to the mastery of magician concentration.

As is well known, the crystal ball is much used by Hindu magicians. Western people often tend to regard the crystal as something mysterious, actually, as used in India, it is not mysterious in the least, it functions entirely as a scientific instrument providing a focusing point for concentration.

The Kandariya Mahadev Temple, located at Khajuraho in Madhya Pradesh State, India. The temple was built during the tenth century by the Rajput kings. It is dedicated to the Hindu god Siva.

Interior carved entirely of white marble of the fabulous Jain Temple located on top of Mt. Abu in Dilwara, Rajasthan, India.

The Hindu teaching strongly advises the initiates to use the crystal as they learn to the art of concentration, and many of the most advanced manifestations of magic are performed by concentrated visualization aided by the crystal ball, as a focal center. Particularly in the training period of the magician is it invariably employed.

The general rule for using the crystal ball by the Yogis is as follows:

(a) Place the crystal either in the palm of the hand, or else place it on a table or stand in front of you. (b) Throw the mind blank by inhibiting sensations and outside thoughts, so that "the lake of the Chitta is free from the ripples of the Vrittis." (c) Gaze intently (but not in a strained manner) into the crystal, at the same time fixing and keeping the mind firmly concentrated upon some particular subject, object, or mental picture.

Basically that is the entirety of the instruction. I shall give you some particular and additional features when we reach the study of visualization, but the above is sufficient for the commencement of training, development, and perfecting of the powers of concentration. Also, I want you to read into my instructions, as we proceed, that the crystal ball is always to be used when the purpose is the focusing of attention and thought. Let the crystal ball be the

pivoting point around which other instructions revolve. Its use is one of the great secrets of oriental magic.

According to the Yoga teachings, the main purpose of concentration is to get the chitta (or mind stuff) closely focused, or gathered together at one particular point in consciousness. In order to do this, the vrittas (or thought disturbances), must be suppressed, and the bosom of the mental lake of chitta must be kept placid and still, except at the one, tiny concentrated point at which the attention and thought are focused by means of the instrument of the crystal. In this way, there is obtained that "unity of consciousness" and "one pointedness of mind" which is so stressed in the Hindu teachings of real magic.

The venerable Patanjali states, "Binding and holding the mind-stuff to a place in fixed attention is the secret of Dharana. And such fixed attention is possible only when the mind is centered upon one particular point or object in space. To this objective, the use of the crystal ball is admirable."

There is nothing metaphysical in the slightest about the oriental practices of concentration and using the crystal ball for this purpose. The training is decidedly practical for developing perfection of the will and thought for the purpose of concentrated visualization. With practice one will achieve the "knack" of fixing and holding in mind the subject, object, idea, or mental-image connected with the purpose in question. With this knack one will be commencing to achieve a mastery of magic.

The Yogi in teaching concentration to an initiate will ask this question, "Can you concentrate?" The man will answer, "Yes or no, or else say that it is very difficult." To which the Yogi will ask, "Can you pay attention to a thing?" To this question, the answer is invariably "Yes." The Yogi will say, "Very good, for Yoga Concentration is attention. If you pay attention to what you do, your mind will be concentrated."

Many who sit down for Yoga Concentration wonder why they do not succeed. How possibly can one expect that a half hour of Yoga meditation and twenty-three-and-a-half-hours of scattering of thought through the day and night will enable you to concentrate correctly during the half hour? You must literally reverse the process, and practice practical, concrete concentration every hour of your active life, instead of adhering to the habit of scattering your thoughts idly about incessantly. Then you will succeed.

To acquire this habit of continuous concentration, you must pay deliberate attention to every thing you do everyday. When you start the practice, possibly it will be made easier at first only to select out a portion of the day's work, and doing that portion give it unflagging attention. Hold your mind under control and do not let it wander from the thing before you. It does not matter what the thing is. It may be adding up a column of figures, or the reading of a book. Anything will do. It is the attention of the mind which is important; not the object before it. Gradually you can increase the portions of your life in which you give real attention to things. In time, the giving of complete attention will become your habit of thought, and you will then be on your way of learning Yoga Concentration which makes possible the power of concentration.

Parimal Bandhu offers these practical suggestions for training concentration: "Fix your mind rigidly on the work before you for the time being, and when you are done with it, drop it. Practice steadily this method of doing things, and in a surprisingly short time you will find that it will become your natural way, and the concentration of the mind—in attention—will become a habit.

"Or suppose you are an intelligent person fond of reasoning; in this the main exercising of your mind will have been the connecting link of thought and argument. Utilize this past training, but do not imagine that you can make your mind still by a single effort. Follow a logical chain of reasoning, step by step, link after link, and do not allow the mind to swerve a hairs breath from it. Do not allow the mind to go aside to other lines of thought. Keep it rigidly along a single line, and steadiness will gradually result. Then, when you have worked up to your highest point of reasoning, and reached the last link of your chain of argument, and your mind will carry you no further, and beyond which you can see nothing—THEN STOP. Hold fast to that last link of the chain, and keep the mind poised, in steadiness and strenuous quiet, waiting for what may come.

The Chauragash or "Trident Shrine," located 4000 feet in the Rachmarhi Range at Medhya Pradesh. One of the most unique shrines in the world where it is said that Lord Shiva, being pursued by Daemons (the Bhasmarsura) ran for safety, dropped his trident, and hid in a cave. Devotees bring tridents here and deposit them for eternity. It is believed that to remove a trident from this sacred spot of the Hindus is to court perpetual evil. (Courtesy the Prof. S. C. Bose Collection, India)

"Or suppose you are one in which imagination is stronger than the reasoning faculty. In such instance, imagination rather than reasoning will be your method of developing powers of concentration. To this end, picture some scene in which the object of your ideal forms the central figure; built it up in your mind, bit by bit, as a painter creates a picture by gradually putting in all the elements of the scene. Work at it as an artist works on his canvas, line by line, your brush being the brush of imagination. At first the process may be slow, but the picture will soon begin to be formed at call. Over and over again you should picture the scene, dwelling less and less on the surrounding objects, and more and more on the central ideal figure. The drawing of the mental picture in this way, brings it under control and steadies it, and thus gradually by the use of imagination, you bring the mind under command.

"These are suggestions for developing powers of concentration that I have given my students. Practice of this sort builds up the qualities you want, and you become stronger and better fit to proceed onward in your mastery of magic."

These suggestions by the Sadhu I have found most helpful. You will too, and remember, also, to apply them in connection with using the crystal ball, i.e., fix the gaze upon the crystal, "throw the mind blank," and then apply the concentrated attention upon the object of the thought; using reasoning or imagination, as the case may be. In daily performance, you will be using the methods of increasing your attention throughout all waking hours, and use the crystal when you have private opportunities to advance most markedly your mastering of Yoga Concentration.

In relation to the method of using the crystal, perhaps I should give you a little more explanation as to just what is meant in "throwing the mind blank" as used in Yoga. This condition of blank mindedness first of all, is not to be considered mere "empty mindedness." It is, rather, a mental condition of confident expectation—of expecting the coming of something which is to fill the blank space of the mind. In the process, the mind is really not "empty," rather it is stilled.

The surface of "the lake of Chitta" has been rendered quiet, placid, and calm; no longer do the waves, ripples, and tiny whirlpools of the vrittis disturb it. The condition is gained by allowing no interfering thought to enter into consciousness, and permitting the senses to perform none of their functions. This is the meaning of "throwing the mind blank," and is a mental state achieved only by practice. When this difficult task is learned, the attention must be fixed, without swerving, upon its objective. As such the mind is prepared for the practice of Yoga Concentration.

Perhaps you will understand better this idea of "holding the mind blank" if you will relate it to the physical act of holding one's breath. You will remember that in both physical condition and mental states there is a state of quietness and stillness, a cessation of active effort, but, at the same time, a state of intense expectancy and readiness to spring into action. As an analogy, it may be said to resemble the state of a coiled-up steel spring, the moment before its release. Or again, it may be thought of as a state resembling the mental and physical condition of a crouching panther the moment before it springs upon its prey. Your thought in understanding this special condition of mind will give you the "knack" of it; and further practice will make you proficient in it.

The succeeding stage in Yoga Concentration which follows immediately the "hold the mind blank" stage, is that of "holding the thought" upon the subject, object, or mental-picture, as the case may be. In this is meant more than appears on the surface, as in this is the Yoga meaning of Concrete Dhyana, in which is realized a peculiar union of subject and object. As this is important, I asked Parimal Bandhu to explain:

"In Dhyana, there comes to the mind the power, as it were, of the flowing in an unbroken current toward that point. In Dhyana you bring the contemplated or concentrated upon object up to your own mental plane of consciousness, and, so to speak, make it actually a form in your mind. Your "mind stuff" thus assumes the actual form of the contemplated object, and has an actual (though but temporary) existence in your chitta. Thus, it becomes unified with you, for the time being, and it is possible to consider it directly, instead of indirectly through the medium of the senses. The object of Dhyana is to unify the mind with an object and to induce unification with the object. So holding the object in mind, it must be concentrated upon to unify the thing with the mind, in which process a sort of 'click' takes place in the mind, and an extraordinary experience is undergone. The 'thing' joins itself to 'you' by a curious internal phenomenon, and you feel 'one' with it. Clearly the sense of duality between you and it will have vanished, and you have this sense of unification.

"What I have described is the power of mind working upon matter, and is a skill of the Masters. In the initiate it perhaps will not be pronounced, still in every case, there will be a trace of the experience—just enough to let you know that it is there and in operation. Do not seek to overdevelop this power; let it develop naturally and without forcing. You can do good work in Yoga Concentration with but a trace of it, and I should add that this sense of "oneness" between thought and object disappears when the concentration is terminated. I have here given you one of the deepest secrets of creative mind magic."

In closing this chapter dealing with the power of concentration, I wish to give you what are known as "The Obstacles to Yoga Concentration" and "The Seven Little Devils Besetting the Yogi." It is well that you know of these, as with their mastery you advance toward magicianhood.

THE OBSTACLES TO YOGA CONCENTRATION

1 *Disease*. If you are diseased you cannot practice Yoga efficiently, for it demands sound health and physical well being.

2 *Apathy of Mind*. You must be alert, active, energetic, and vigorous in your thought.

3 *Doubt and Disbelief*. You must have faith and decision of will. You must believe in your powers, and be able to make up your mind firmly.

4 *Carelessness*. This is for some initiates a great difficulty, as many study carelessly, and perform the exercises inaccurately and inattentively.

5 *Laziness*. A lazy man cannot be a true Yogi, for if one lacks the ambition and will to exert himself, how may he make the exertions required in Yoga?

6 *Worldly-Mindedness and Frivolity*. How may the chaser-after-shadows grasp the reality?

7 *Erroneous Ideas*. Mistaken ideas and wrong thinking lead one from the right path.

8 *Instability*. The purpose, aim, and end of the Yogi must be stable, fixed, constant, persistent, preserving. The unpurposeful man can never be a Yogi.

THE SEVEN LITTLE DEVILS BESETTING THE YOGI

1 *Physical Sensations*. The annoying little disturbing itchings, fatigues, tiredness, etc. which distract the attention of the Yogi from his concentration or meditation. He must learn to refuse them his attention.

2 *Sense Reports*. The sights, sounds, smells, tastes, and touch sensations (stimuli) coming from the outside world, and disturbing the concentrated thought of the Yogi. He must learn to inhibit them, and "shut them out" by denying them his attention.

3 *Memories*. The memory, recollection, or remembrances of past experiences, which disturb the peace and distract the attention of the Yogi. He must learn to deny them his attention.

The Great Stupa at Sanchi. Located five miles from Bhopal, the capital of Madhya Pradesh, India, this shrine is revered by the Buddhists. It preserves the relics of Gautama Buddha's two famous disciples, Sariputta and Moggallana.

4 *Reveries*. The "day dreamings" which intrude upon the restful mind, and distract the attention. The Yogi must divert these by refusing them attention.

5 *Involuntary Thought Analysis*. The subtle, analysis of one's own mental states which tend to come in contemplation and meditation, and which divert the attention from its proper object of concentration. The Yogi must think only about the object of his concentration; not about his thoughts concerning it, or the manner of its performance.

6 *Thought Influence*. Influences coming from other minds. As a sensitive, the Yogi must overcome such subtle "little devils" by resolutely denying them his attention.

7 *Dimmed Consciousness*. The dreamy, sleepy, drowsiness in which consciousness becomes dim, hazy, or clouded. Concentration, contemplation, and meditation must be "wide awake" in the Yogi. One must either go to sleep, or else stay awake, but do not try to combine the two states at the same time.

You have learned of "The Obstacles to Yoga Concentration" and "The Seven Little Devils Besetting the Yogi;" keep them at a distance and out of your field of consciousness; remember that such as these that pertain to the Yogi pertain to the magician.

When you have mastered the art/sciences of Pratyahara, Dharana, and Dhyana—the method of Yoga mental control and concentration, then you will experience that which is spoken of in the ancient knowledge:

"Then will that which you hold in thought be as the strong, steady flame of the light of the temple. Gone will be all flickerings, all waverings, all sputtering. The winds which once disturbed it will have died down and finally ceased; and no longer will the insects plunge into its flame and disturb its steadiness. Then will the lamp be worthy of its flame, and the flame worthy of its lamp, and both worthy of the high priest of the temple, which is your real self."

8

Oriental Visualization and Projection

You have now learned how to develop your source of energy for the performance of magic. You have also learned how to concentrate the powers of the mind and associate mind with matter. You will now learn the next step in the magical arts—the power of visualization and through projection.

Common to all forms of magic is the custom of the magician to first form a mental picture of the thing or event he wishes to have become materialized into a physical reality. The process is known as visualization.

Visualization is employed in all phases of the real magic of India to an advanced degree, the power being used as Maya (which will be studied in this chapter and in further detail in subsequent chapters of this book) in which the visualization—of his feats—in the mind of the magician is projected as an image to appear as real to the minds of the spectators. This is a most startling form of oriental magic. It is the intermediate magic, and it is important that you become familiar with these principles as the means through which these processes may be manifested and demonstrated.

As explained in the Hindu teachings, maya is a manifestation of mind based upon principles which you have already studied, namely, (1) Akasha, the ethereal material principle; (2) Prana, the subtle principle of energy; (3) Creative Mind, the principle of creative idealization. The ancient teachings hold that the entire Universe is the product of the action and reaction, combination and correlation of these three basic principles of nature; above which abides the soul, which in the human being is represented by the ego, "I," or real self.

In the performance of this magic, the stronger the magician is able to create his visualizations in mind, the more powerful will be the effects produced in the physical world. Accordingly, the main training of the intermediate magicians is along this line of visualization and thought projection, in which training the crystal ball is universally employed for the development of the powers just as it is used in processes of Yoga Concentration.

Intensified imagination, coupled with intensive will, then, is seen to be the twin-instrument of the Hindu magic power of Maya, viz., the intensified imagination first creating the mental picture (or visualization), which the intensive will then holds in a firm state, and finally projects it in the desired direction. This projected mental-picture then materializing in one or both of the following two general ways:

1   It creates in the chitta of another, or other persons, a tiny reproduction of its own form, thus making the other person, or persons, think and see the things so visualized and projected.

2   It creates in the akasha, an *astral or psychic picture* which reproduces the original visualized mental image, and thus makes the latter *seem to be real* to the minds of other persons.

In the first of these forms of manifestation, the reproduction of the visualization in the chitta (or "mind stuff") of others persons is found the underlying explanation of what has been called "Oriental Hypnotism" or "Psychic Influencing." This is Maya with which you are familiar.

In the second of these forms of manifestion of magic, i.e., the reproduction of the visualization in the akasha will be found the explanation of many wonderful feats of the advanced Hindu magicians such as "The Fast Indian Rope Trick," the levitation of a human body, or whatever fanciful illusion the magician is able to imagine, in which large numbers of spectators seem actually to "see" certain happenings which have no real existence outside of the mind of the magician.

In many forms of magic, however, it should be remembered that there is really a combination of these two forms of manifestation performed simultaneously. The same effort of the magician's mind produces both forms and both effects, so there is really no need to attempt to dissect one from the other. In fact, instead of being two distinct forms, they may be stated more accurately as being "the major and minor phases," respectively, of the same fundamental and essential thing.

To emphasize the explanation of the process, the magician in projecting a powerful mental-picture to a number of persons, often, more or less unconsciously, *also* sets up an "astral picture" or "thought form" in the ethereal substance of the akasha, which then reflects itself upon the chitta or "mind stuff" of many other persons. In like manner, the magician in projecting a powerful "thought form" in the akasha, often, without any additional effort, *also* causes that "astral picture" to be reflected into the chitta of many other persons. The process is thus seen as one of constant action and reaction; a constant coordination, combination, and correlation between these two great general forms of manifestation.

All of the previously described instructions of the Yoga methods for the performance of magic, which you have studied, have as their chief end, in this regard, the cultivation, development, and training of The Power Of Visualization and Projection—those twin-elements of magic and psychic power. If you wish to attain a high degree of proficiency in performing the real magic, you must possess to a high degree the power of visualization and projection; and in order to possess these extraordinary talents of the mind, you must first have mastered the Yoga methods of mental control. As such, your aim is that of the Adept, the master magician.

However one does not need to become an Adept in order to begin the performance of mental magic. Even without perfection you can begin to manifest to a surprisingly high degree; although, of course, you will do well to develop and perfect yourself as your training advances. Indeed, you will unquestionably wish to do so as you will find your desire for greater power increasing in proportion to your successful manifestations of the magic/psychic power in lesser degree. You need not wait for this, however; you may start in at once, and begin to manifest and demonstrate your increasing power as you proceed. You should be able to obtain some quite satisfactory results and effects even from the start, provided that you proceed properly and intelligently, with perseverance and persistency.

I shall now give you the oriental teaching concerning visualization and projection. Remember, what you are reading is as scientific data to the magician just as the reading of a text on mathematics would be to a western scientist. So study it in like manner, giving it your scholarly attention.

PRELIMINARY STAGES

Before commencing the practices for developing powers of visualization and projection, it is recommended that you initially prepare yourself for the subsequent mental exertion by a few preliminary observations. In this regard, rest yourself mentally and physically for a little time before commencing your practice. Take tension off your body and strain off your mind, and try to "let go" for a few moments, until you feel the sense of poise and calmness that such relaxation brings.

Also it is recommended that the initiate perform some of the refreshing and invigorating exercises in rhythmic breathing that you have learned. Use those that bring you a sense of restful power.

You are now ready for your practice session in visualization and projection.

USING THE CRYSTAL BALL

First of all, rid your mind of all beliefs that there is some miraculous power inherent in the crystal as used by magicians. The crystal ball is simply an efficient instrument or device serving as a focal center in which to focus and concentrate your mental forces in the process of visualization. Regard the crystal ball in your work precisely as a scientist would regard the lens of his microscope or telescope. In your work, the crystal operates akin to a magnifying glass which in focusing the rays of the sun can generate enough heat to cause a fire; the crystal ball focuses the currents of the mental energy in a similar manner.

Secondly, remove any fantastic ceremonies from your crystal practices in visualization. It is true that some of the Hindu magicians surround their work with the crystal ball with mystical proceedings, but such are entirely psychological in nature; you do not need them. However, there does seem to be a sort of "polarization" of the crystal as the result of the mental energy directed

The Juma Masjid. Built by the great Shan Jehan at Delhi in A.D. *1650, it is revered by t. Muslims and is the largest mosque in India.*

toward it. Thus the crystal will tend to work better for the individual the longer he or she uses it. To this end, it is advised that you keep the crystal ball you use exclusively for your own work, and do not allow it to be used by others.

You may obtain a crystal ball at any supply house of magical apparatus. A solid glass ball three or four inches in diameter is fine. Be sure the glass is clear and free from flaws, as such are distracting.

Following are the rules for using the crystal effectively in your practice of visualization.

1   As much as possible, have the room in which you practice crystal visualization quiet and free from disturbing outside sights and sounds. Also, it is well to have it furnished simply, and remove all mirrors. The general color tone of the room should be subdued, and it should be comfortable in temperature. Have the room lighted in a low key when you practice; in other

words, use moderate lighting that is neither too bright or too dark. In placing the crystal in the room, arrange it so that the rays of light do not reach it directly, nor be reflected in or from it. The light source should always be from behind your back, and never in front of you.

2   The crystal ball may either rest on its stand, or unsupported on the table placed in front of you, or you may, if you prefer, hold it Yogi style in the palm of your hand. Many occultists favor having the crystal resting on a black velvet cushion, and have its immediate surroundings likewise in black.

3   In concentrating upon the crystal (the term gazing is used by the Seers), you should never strain or overly fatigue your eyes. Instead, you should maintain a calm, restful gaze. Remember, you are to gaze at the crystal, not to stare at it. Do not try to avoid blinking your eyes; be completely natural in the practice. Do not become impatient, excited, or anxious in learning the skill, and do not treat it as a game. You are learning to use a scientific instrument of the occult; be serious about it. You may also make two funnels of your hands, gazing through them at the crystal as you would through a pair of opera glasses. Yogis often advise this technique to initiates.

4   Perform your practice with the crystal ball when you are alone. Other persons present can be most disturbing. Solitude is an aid to concentration.

5   Acquire proficiency in using the crystal gradually, make your sessions no longer than ten minutes each, at the start. After a time, this period may be

Sculpture on Gopuram, Minakshi Amman Temple, Madurai, Southern India. This magnificent temple is dedicated to the goddess Minakshi, the consort of the Great Lord Shiva. The Ceremony of the Sundareswarar is celebrated here annually. Courtesy Archaeological Survey of India.

increased to fifteen minutes. Later on, the period may be lengthened to thirty minutes, and so on. But, when the period-time of one hour is reached, you should impose the final time limit at that point. I do not advise sittings in crystal concentration for over one hour each for persons in the occident.

6   Your success in using the crystal does not in any way depend upon your ability to see pictures "in" the crystal, as many seek in what is called "crystal gazing." This is not your purpose in this practice; your purpose is that of creating a clear, strong mental-picture in the focused and concentrated "mind"—not in the crystal. The mental-picture is to be seen in "the mind's eye," as it were, and not by the physical eye as a reflection in the crystal. The visualization is in "that which is the inner eye which is the bliss of solitude," as it is expressed in India. Visualization is difficult to some persons, while easy to others. There is a certain "knack" required to master the process, but this will come to all with practice and gradual development.

7   If you find you have difficulty in visualizing at first, you will do well to begin systematically to cultivate the ability of "seeing in the mind's eye"— using the crystal to accomplish this. Begin by trying to "see" in your imagination some simple object like a chair, table, or some other uncompli- cated object with which you are familiar. Then proceed to more complex and difficult objects.

Rather than trying to create the object directly in the mind, go about it indirectly, by imagining that you are looking at a painted or printed picture of the object. As you advance on to more complicated objects, you can view them as if you were seeing such on a screen as an imaginary motion picture. Many students find this approach to visualizing helpful.

Another device that is useful in cultivating the ability of "seeing in the mind's eye" is to simply hold the thought of the thing, object, condition, or objective without actually trying to completely visualize it in picture form. Some people find this easier than forming mental-pictures. Many Hindu magicians use this method exclusively with excellent results, as in the last analysis a mental-picture is but "a thought made visible." In all cases, the crystal ball is used as the focal point of the thought idea.

8   Finally, in all practices of operations with the crystal ball you should observe the Yogi rule of "throwing the mind blank" before proceeding to visualize. The mental slate must be wiped off and cleaned, before any new drawing is placed upon it. The magicians express it in a variety of ways, such as: the mental lake must be still, before new ripples or waves of the vrittis are created in it; the mental metal must be rendered fluid, before it is poured into new molds; the old buildings must be torn down, and the ground cleared, before new buildings may be erected in the same area. This fundamental rule of oriental magic and/or psychic power must never be lost sight of.

THE OBJECTS OF VISUALIZATION

The object of visualization, to the magician or occultist, is always this: That which the magician desires to have become materialized, objectified, and actualized in physical form and action in the world of the physical plane.

Under this general classification come things, qualities, powers, persons, events, happenings, conditions, circumstances, and environment. Indeed, everything, in fact, that can be desired and wished for, on the one hand, or else dreaded and avoided, on the other.

Dread, fear, dislike, and aversion, you must always remember, are but negative forms of desire, and their objects are as much subject to the laws of visualization and materialization as are the positive forms. That "the things I have feared, have come upon me," is quite as true as that "as a man thinketh, so is he." In both instances, the visualization accompanied the thought, and sets into operation the natural laws of mental materialization. Beware of visualizing the things you fear, dread, or desire to avoid!

Always make the objective of your visualization positive in aspect, of benefit, and worthy of desire. Follow these seven principles in applying concentrated visualization as you proceed to mentally create the things you desire to become materialized in objective form, condition, state, and activity, viz.:

The Great Merlin (Merlin Mystery Show) performaing a crystal grazing act Hindu style. Mental-Magic demonstrations have become very popular in the repertoire of modern stage magicians.

Merlin assisted by Erna in their Hindu Mystery Show.

1   Visualize the desired things, events, happenings, circumstances, conditions, and actions just as you wish them to be and become; always seeing them "in your mind's eye" as if they were present in actual reality here and now.

2   Thus, in like manner, visualize yourself as you wish to be or to do.

3   Thus, in like manner, visualize others as you wish them to be or to do.

4   Thus, in like manner, visualize conditions and circumstances as you wish them to be or become.

5   Thus, in like manner, visualize your environment and surrounding as you wish them to be or become.

5   Thus, in like manner, visualize your environment and surrounding as you wish them to be or to become.

6   Thus, in like manner, visualize happenings and events as you wish them to occur.

7   Finally, thus and in like manner, always visualize yourself as possessing and manifesting powers, ability, and strength which you desire and wish to possess and manifest.

On studying this listing of the seven principles of objectives of visualization, you will discover that it includes everything that you might wish or desire to be materialized as a physical reality, which to the magician means that everything one desires and wishes to become real may be made to become so by mental magic and psychic force   provided the principles manifested are applied correctly and efficiently. Such is what the magicians and occultists do when they "make magic," as the term goes.

In developing as a real magician, always bear in mind that the two great elements of mental magic and occult power are (1) Visualization, or mental-picturing, and (2) Projection by the will.

PROJECTION BY THE WILL

We will now study the second element of mental magic, that of "projection." By projection is meant the propelling impulse of the will by means of which the visualized mental-picture is sent forth, discharged, or projected into the outer world from the mind of the magician. The projection may be toward the mind of some particular person; toward the "amalgamated mind" of a crowd, or masses of people; or toward the akasha, with the purpose of materializing upon its screen the psychic picture reproducing or representing the original visualization.

Projection is essentially a process of will; an act of will. A strong thought held in the mind always tends to be projected, but the trained magician does not depend alone on this inherent power of the will. Instead, he adds to this inherent power by deliberate effort and action of his will. This power to deliberately mentally project is complicated in explanation but surprisingly simple in operation. It might be said that it is easily performed once you have "the knack of it." And, this knack consists in simply and coolly making up your mind to project the thought, and then "willing to will" its projection. It is a mental act similar to that which you manifest when you "will" to take a step, to raise your

The Gopuram to the Temple of Madurai. This magnificent gateway shows carvings of Krishna and scenes of Ramayama. In the detailed friezes are depicted many legends revered by the Hindus showing Rama, his consort Sita and brother Lakshmana, and other devotee figures. (From the S. C. Bose Collection)

hand, to strike a blow, or to perform any other kind of physical act; or when you "will" to fix and hold your attention upon anything.

In the mental act of psychic projection you "will" in such a way as might be likened to "pulling the trigger of the will" or releasing the "will's spring of action." The action is really a "release" or "letting go" of the confined, restrained, tense energy. The blow of the fist, the projected bullet from a rifle,

98

the words which explode from your mouth spontaneously as the result of tensed thought—all these are illustrative of this released energy.

In projection following visualization you make the little "extra push" of the will, and thus "shoot out" the thought from your mind like a bullet from a rifle. Some magicians send it out in currents of force flowing from the eyes; others project it like the projection of a motion picture upon a screen. The more powerfully you can mentally sense the "seeing and feeling" of the out-going flow of the projection, the more effective will be the projection by the will.

The Yogis greatly strengthen the power of projection by deliberately energizing the thought with prana, and sending it forth in projection by adding the charge of prana to the will-effort. This process of energizing and charging with prana is purely a mental act, and requires simply (1) the realization that a supply of prana is available for the purpose, and (2) the thought or idea that the visualization is being energized by prana, and that the "will projection" is charged with prana. In other words, it may be said that the mere realization and thought of the process is sufficient to effect the energization and charging of pranic power.

The ability to use prana in this way may be cultivated by the practice of visualizing such action on the part of prana, and you can use special sessions in your visualization practices for this purpose. In such you are following the path of the magician in developing power; in such development exercises you create a familiar "mental path" over which the mind will travel during the times of actual thought projection. The process will in time become a habit of mind, a subconscious reaction and performance. In performing such exercises aimed at this objective, always "see" and "feel" the inflow of prana and its outflow in projection. In this way, you establish an automatic absorption and discharging of prana by the mind that results in a willed projection of power.

99

9

The Magic of Words and Sound

There is a further basic power of the magicians that you must now study. It is called Mantra-Yoga, and is considered an important part of Yoga teaching which is concerned with the use of words and sounds in magical manifestations.

Incantations have always had a part in magical practice, much of which is based on superstition, but the Yogis in the performance of Mantra-Yoga look behind the surface usage of words and verses as "charms" calculated to work wonders, and search out the true scientific principles underlying the use of words and sounds in a magical way. In Mantra-Yoga they offer careful instruction in the efficient employment of such words and sounds for the purpose of obtaining the most powerful psychological results that influence.

As a magician initiate you must learn of Mantra-Yoga.

Mantrams hold two meanings to the Hindus, one that is religious and one that is magical. The latter pertains to our particular interest in this book. The occult definition of mantrams alludes to: "A definite succession of sounds, repeated over and over again in succession, which synchronizes the chitta or 'mind stuff' " or "A series of words uttered rhythmically for the purpose of concentrated meditation."

Throughout all history, "the spoken word" has held a prominent place in ceremonies of magic. The masses interpret such as being in the nature of charms and incantations possessing magical power in themselves, but the inner magical teaching shows their true power to be mainly psychological in nature. "Affirmations" in magic affirm the power of the spoken word, and have been used by mystics for ages. It is a complicated subject, yet an important one to the magician, so I asked Sadhu Parimal Bandu to explain the matter in relation to the magic of India. These are the Avatar's comments:

"I will give you a variety of concepts from which you may draw knowledge of this subject. Look again upon the chitta, as the stilled lake of mind-stuff, ready for pulsation to come upon its surface, and hear in words and sounds their

A teeming market in a village in India. In places such as this is seen the wonderful native magic of India.

Performing magicians in India. These are the famous Banjara mystifiers of Andhra Pradesh, who are extremely popular in India.

basic vibration which can form ripples upon the lake. As soon as that sound enters your ears, there is a corresponding wave of the vrittis produced in your chitta along with that sound of the word. Let us say that the wave of vrittis in the chitta represents the idea of a 'cow,' the form or meaning as you know it. That apparent 'cow' that you know is really that wave in the chitta or mind-stuff, and that comes as a reaction to the internal and external sound vibrations, and with the sound waves dies away.

"Or it can be expressed this way, in looking upon mantras as a series of words uttered rhythmically. Such series of words are developed formula which have been worked out by the Hindu masters, and the effect of these words on the body is to produce a certain result. The power of these words seems to create a sort of rhythm in the body which is quite remarkable. And, if I were to speak along the line of a western psychologist, I can add, also, that words, in themselves, have a power, meaning, suggestive and/or autosuggestive effect upon the mental states; the aroused mental state then producing the decided effect upon the body. In many cases, the virtue is found not to abide alone in 'the spoken word,' but rather in the mental state aroused by the latter.

"I will likewise call your attention to the fact that your being is restless; it is in constant motion, and every vibration of the being produces a corresponding change in the consciousness. The mantram provides a way to check the constant vibration of being into unity, then consciousness may be stilled. Accordingly, look upon mantram as a mechanical way of stilling the body, and through the body the mind. In other words, instead of using mental powers, you save these for other purposes, and use mantram for stilling the being."

Here in these words of the Sadhu, you have the three fundamental secrets of the powers of mantrams, (1) in the vibratory elements of a certain cadence of sounds, and (2) in the suggestion/autosuggestion effects arising from the meaning of the words, which in creating certain mental states tend to set into operation the powers of the mind, (3) in a mechanical method of "stilling" the being. These are all important factors to an understanding of mantrams and the power of words in relation to successful magic.

It is interesting to observe that not only are mantrams found in Hinduism, but in Buddhism, in Roman Catholicism, and among the Moslems. In all of these widely divergent practitioners of mantrams, it is held that a mantram cannot be translated, for when the specific succession and order of the sounds, for which it has been designed, is altered, the mantram is destroyed. In this, we find an explanation of the importance of the correct handling and saying of "magic words," spells, and incantations by the magician if such are to be effective in some types of magics.

While mantras are frequently used in conjunction with religious cere-monies, there is nothing particularly religious about them. Mantra is a power which lends itself impartially to any use. Mantras have been used in many types of ceremonies, and in various types of magic from black to white. In relation to Yoga, it is an inspiring influence, and is expressed as being thought—movement vehicled—by and expressed—in speech. The Yogis say, "Mantras provide an objective means of arousing Kundalini. The substances of all mantras is feeling-consciousness."

102

In my personal study of mantrams, I am inclined to regard them as a sort of "energized thoughts" or "vitalized ideas" expressed in words charged with power. I feel that it will be found that the essence of the powers of mantras will be recognized as being in the energized and vitalized thought or idea inherent in the words; the words themselves being but the form.

The vibrations are in the thoughts and feelings, not alone in the sounds, or form of the words. In music, the sounds, cadences and such forms of expression undoubtedly arouse feelings and emotion in us—there can be no doubt of that. But, is it not equally true that these sounds and musical measures are, in themselves, but representations in outward form of feelings and emotions which were previously in the souls of those who composed them. Ask yourself this question, "What do we mean when we say that a musician 'puts soul into his music,' or that a composer has 'expressed his soul' in his composition?"

I am sure you appreciate the point in this showing that the original essence and spirit of the mantrams, as of music, are in the mind, feelings, or soul of the human being who designed them. Thus, these words, phrases, verses, sounds when repeated in mantrams and heard by other persons tend to arouse and awaken similar and corresponding feelings, emotion and mental states in them. All feelings, emotions, and other mental states have unquestionably a magic or psychical power. This magic or psychic power, aroused and directed by the mantras, is that power which some students seek to attribute directly to the vibration of the words.

Swami Vivekananda says, "Repeating the Vedas, and other Mantrams, by which the Sattva material in the body is purified, is called Svadhyaya. There are three sorts of repetitions of mantrams. One is called verbal; another semi-verbal; the third mental. The verbal or audible is the lowest, while the inaudible (mental) is the highest of all. The repetition which is so loud that anybody can hear it, is the verbal. The next one is where the vocal organs only begin to vibrate, but no sound is heard. One might say that this is verbal but of a type where another man sitting near cannot hear what is said. The third and highest is the mental repetition of the mantram, at the same time thinking of its meaning. This is called 'mental muttering' and is of great power."

There is profound knowledge in the above statements, audible mantram being placed in the lowest classification, partially audible mantram in the intermediate, and mentally repeated mantram in the highest. The concept is obviously that the real virtue of mantras abides in the thought, feeling, and idea rather than in the mere verbal form or sound expressing them.

Of the verbalized Hindu mantrams, the paramount form is expressed in the syllable, "OM!" This is regarded as a highly sacred mantra, and I will have more to say about it in a moment. Other sacred matras used in India are "Om, Tat, Sat Om" meaning "O Thou Self-existent One," and "Tat Avam Asi" meaning "That Thou Art."

The Buddhists, in like manner, have their favorite mantram in their familiar "Om Mani Padme, Hum" meaning "Oh, Jewel of the Lotus, Amen." The Mohammadens have their sacred mantram in "La Allah illa Allah" meaning "Allah is the only God." And in relation to religious mantras, the "Hail Mary" of the Catholic Church has high reverence.

103

The sacred syllable of "Om" is considered by the Hindus to be the mantram of mantrams. They regard it in reverence in Mantra-Yoga, and state, "The manifesting word of the supreme Purusha is Om!" There is a mantram termed the Gayatri which is a holy verse from the Vedas, it reads: "We meditate upon the glory of that Being who has produced this universe; may He enlighten our minds." To this Gayatri, the syllable, "Om" is joined at the beginning and the end.

Yogis in the practicing of Pranayama will repeat three Gayatris, beginning and ending with the syllable, "Om"—using certain symbolical words, instead of counting "one, two, three, four, five, six" in pranayama breathing. In your own practice of Pranayama, it is well that you join the mental repetition of the word "Om" to the Pranayama. Let the sacred word flow in and out with the breath, rhythmically and harmoniously. It will add a rhythm to your being.

Sadhu Bandu, says, "Around this word 'Om' are centered all the different religious sects of India, and all of the various religious ideas expressed in the Vedas are gathered in this one word. It has around it various significances, which can be accepted by everyone, east or west. Remember, one moment of company with that which is Holy makes a ship to cross the ocean of life. So in the repetition of 'Om' and thinking of its meaning, you are keeping good company in your mind. Study and then meditate, and meditate when you have studied. Thus light will come to you, and the self will become manifest. One must think of this 'Om' and its meaning too; the first manifestation of this repetition and thinking of "Om" will be that the introspective power of your mind will be manifested more and more, and all mental and physical obstacles will begin to vanish."

You will note that the Sadhu emphasized the "thinking of the meaning" of the mantram, in connection with its repetition. All through the study of Mantra-Yoga is found the inevitable combination of repetition and thinking, which is the inner secret of the use of mantrams.

It is not to be wondered at that, that the sacred mantram of "Om" (pronounced "AUM") will have a most powerful psychological effect upon the mind of anyone understanding the significance of the thought expressed in the term. It expresses the thought of the One Supreme Power in the Universe, which is held to be mirrored in the soul of the individual just as the Sun is mirrored in the falling rain-drops or in the drops of dew gathered upon the leaf of the Lotus. It is held that meditation upon this ONE in Om will bring the light in the dew drop in touch with the light of the Sun. The mantram of mantras will arouse mind, thought, emotion, feeling, and will to their highest stages of power, all of which are objectives of the magician. It brings into being the psychical energies of man.

Ohashnuhara, in teaching of Yoga, writes, "In the pronunciation of 'Om' as 'AUM' the effect will be found to be instantaneous and little short of magical. The vibration of this sound arouses the body, setting the whole system atingle until the polarization of the body is altered, and, of course, purification from an occult standpoint is achieved.

"The vibrations aroused are so powerful that they shut out all self-influence, attracting the finer and purer influences, sounds and vibrations which will awaken the occult forces possessed by the student, making him a new

104

Ritual to the Lord Rama during the Diwali Festival (The Festival of Lights). Every home is lit up with little oil lamps. It is an occasion for great rejoicing, and marks both the return of Lord Rama to his kingdom after fourteen years in exile in the forest and the beginning of the new year.

and infinitely more powerful being; the power to attract good from all things and to find good in all things.

"But I must warn, do not pronounce the sacred word except when your thoughts are pure and your desires are holy, and never utter it in flippant company. Remember, the sound when working in the harmonious, builds, but when working in the inharmonious tends to destroy. Everything that is pure is harmonious and attracts the good; while that which is impure is inharmonious and attracts the opposite pole."

As has been mentioned, the correct pronunciation of the Hindu Sacred Mantram is always "Aum." The "Aum" sound consisting of three sound-elements, each shading into the one following it, the last sound being a decreasing hum. The "Ah" shades into the "Oo," and the latter dies away in the decreasing and long-drawn-out final "Mmmm" or humming sound proceeding from the closed lips. The combined sound is that of "Ahhh-oooo-mmmmm." The mantram is best sounded by the exhaling breath of a cycle of rhythmic breathing. The breath, however, should be exhaled through the mouth, instead of the nostrils.

As Sadhu Parimal Bandu explained it, "OM (Aum) is a fundamental sound. The first letter, A, (pronounced 'Ah') is the root sound, the key, pronounced without touching any part of the tongue or palate. The second letter, U, (pronounced 'Oo') rolls from the very root of the end of the sounding board of the mouth. The third and final letter, M, (pronounced 'Mmm') represents the final sound of the series, being produced through closed lips. The student should dwell upon the final M, making it vibrate in the throat like the hum of a bee, prolonging the sound for as long as he is able to do on the one inhalation. Thus OM (Aum) represents a large gamut of sound production by human beings. It may be considered as a matrix of speech, and denotes the basic sound foundation for a wide range of words that can be spoken."

In Yoga, the three letters of the sacred A-U-M signify the principles of the creation. *A* signifies preservation, *U* signifies destruction, and *M* signifies regeneration. To the Hindus, the Wayshowers of Brahma, Vishnu and Shiva are represented in this. In the same manner of symbolism are the three-fold elements of Nature, as are also represented the three states of consciousness. The Yogi says that as the vibrations of the sacred word speed faster, he is carried in spirit to the divine centers of his being, the power of vibration pierces the material nature of his being, and by transition through his subjective mind it reaches the eternal principle within his heart and awakens it to life.

Of such is the Mantram of Mantras—the Sacred Word—the OM of the Yogis. It is submitted for your consideration, and it is suggested that one never lose sight of the fact that the inner element of the mantram is the thought or idea sought to be expressed in it; that is the"soul" of the power generated by it, the outer element or verbal form being merely the "shell" within which lies the kernal of the process. The power so evoked is "mental power," and not merely the physical power of sound-vibrations; the effective vibrations being mental vibrations, not physical ones. As mentioned, such is the inner secret of Mantra-Yoga.

106

AFFIRMATIONS AND VERBAL STATEMENTS

The principle of the mantrams may be applied to more familiar applications and manifestations of the creative power of the mind. It has been said, "Words are crystallized thoughts." And, the repetitions of certain suggestive words serves to strengthen, render positive and effective the thought or idea behind them. Thus, if you are employing creative thought in a certain direction, as for instance, in the process of visualization, you can strengthen the mental-picture by actually "saying" the thing that you are visualizing; the verbal expression serving to crystalize the visualization. It also serves to direct pranic energy to the latter, animating it. Thus, the philosophy of Emerson, "Brace yourself with affirmations."

Not only in the phase of visualization may the process of Creative Mind be intensified by means of proper affirmations or verbal statements, the same method may also be applied with benefit to the phase of projection in the same process. You will find, by actual experiment and practice, that there is a definite "projective" force added to thought, feeling, idea, or mental-picture by a strong verbal expression thereof. In this action, the effort and action of the will manifesting itself in expression tends to communicate itself to the propulsion or projection of the mental-form into the outer world. Especially in relationship between individuals may the element of affirmation or verbal statement be added with profit and efficiency. The action is twofold in making stronger the visualization and its subsequent projection, and also serving to carry the mental-message and will-determination to the recepient.

In occult treatises of magical processes, the magician is almost always presented as "saying" or making verbal statements of the creative acts that follow. Reference to the miraculous powers of the spoken word may also be found in the Holy Scriptures. As for example in Genesis, Jehovah is pictured as saying, "Let there be light!" And the Scriptures continues, ". . . and there was light!" Again, "God said, 'Let there be a firmament, in the midst of the waters, and let it divide the waters from the waters." And so it was accomplished, as it was verbalized.

In employing this principle of affirmation or verbal statement in relation to the performance of magic, keep in mind the statement of Swami Vivekananda in which he reminds his pupils that the highest form of mantra is that in which there is no utterance by the voice, but in which there is rather a "mental muttering" accompanied by a "thinking of the meaning." The vocal mantram is too apt to dissipate its power in mere sound. The subtle mentally-uttered mantram, on the other hand, conserves its power and energy, and employs it in the *mental projection and psychic propulsion*. In this handling, the words are converted into "bullets" of energy saturated by prana, instead of being "shot" of lifeless verbal material. Used thus, we have the true magic of words.

You have now learned of the magic power of words (affirmations). In the next chapter, I will show you Initiate Demonstrations in Personal Psychic Influencing using affirmations, as you learn the art of Maya.

A Hindu Kirtan the singfest of mantrams. To most it is but verbal mantra, but to some it develops into a psychic experience of deep meaning. Remember, the highest of mantrams is the mental mantram which is not uttered by the voice but is "mentally muttered."

A native performer of Maya.

10
Learning the Art of Maya

You have learned of the methods of developing the powers of the magicians. I will now show you how to use these powers in performance. In this chapter, you will learn how to produce Maya, which is the magician's way of influencing the minds of others.

The Hindu magicians are past masters in the art of psychic influencing. They have studied this art for hundreds of years, and skill in maya is handed down from teacher to pupil; the initiate faithfully practicing the art throughout his life. It is little wonder that the Hindu magicians become remarkably skilled in the performance of maya, and are able to produce results in mentally influencing people which seems to be miraculous to persons unfamiliar with the natural laws underlying the phenomena.

Maya has been called Oriental Hypnotism. It is related most closely to what western psychologists refer to as "waking suggestion" or "waking hypnosis," as it does not require the formal induction of the special mental state of hypnosis. The Yogis refer to it as the direct psychic control of the imagination and will of other persons. This is the power claimed to be used by the intermediate magicians of India for the performance of their spectacular illusions; illusions of mystery that occur within the minds of the observers.

Before proceeding to the explanation of the principles and methods used in performing maya, it is well that you observe how this form of psychic influencing differs from that known in the West as mesmerism and hypnotism respectively.

Mesmerism was the forerunner of hypnotism as it is known in western countries. It was the term employed to designate the teaching and methods of Dr. Anton Frederick Mesmer, who lived in Vienna in 1775. His practices bear his name. He threw people into a sleeplike condition, and produced effects upon them by means of what he called "animal magnetism," which he described as a sort of universal fluid claiming it to flow from himself to other people with curative effects. In action, it was akin to physical magnetism. He was a sensation in Europe, and attracted great attention during his lifetime. Mesmer is regarded as one of the early pioneers in psychotherapy.

109

Hypnotism is a term created by Dr. James Braid, a surgeon of Manchester, England. He coined it from the Greek word, "hypnos," meaning sleep, and used it to differentiate his work. Dr. Braid achieved much prominence during the early part of the last century, and he is regarded as "the father of modern hypnotism." He consider his method of practice as different from Mesmer's, and introduced it as a new discovery.

Braid's method was to produce an unusual physiological condition by the staring at an object; the object being held before the center of the forehead, the two eyes being turned upward to a central point of fixation, thus producing a condition of strain. After tiring out the patient in this way, Dr. Braid put him into a sleep-like condition (which has subsequently become known as hypnosis), and then caused him to perform certain actions as the result of verbal commands or suggestions.

Braid, himself, regarded his induced state as a purely physiological one and did not attach particular importance to the psychological factor of suggestion. It was for the celebrated French Schools of Hypnotic Suggestion to advance the idea that the real manifesting force in the phenomena consisted of the suggestions, or "induced imagination," produced in or upon the patient by the statements and commands of the hypnotist. Even the "sleep condition," itself, was finally seen to result from the psychological factor of suggestion rather than a physiological one, as Braid proposed. Still his name for the state persisted, so the idea of "hypnotic sleep" became inseparable from hypnosis.

Only in relatively recent years has psychology gradually worked away from the idea of the complete necessity of the "sleep condition" to achieve effective results from suggestion. Suggestion in definition is stated as being a subconscious realization of an idea. In other words, one might say that suggestion is the impressing of a thought, idea, or feeling (usually verbalized) upon the mind of a person so that it is responded to unconsciously (automatically). Hypnosis is still regarded as a mental condition in which suggestions produce their greatest effects, but it is now appreciated that even without hypnosis suggestions possess potent power.

The Oriental magicians based their practice of hypnotism (which they term, Maya, or psychic influencing) upon the principle that "the will follows the imagination, and the imagination is susceptible to psychic influence." They proceed with their work of direct psychic influencing as follows:

1 The magician (call him oriental hypnotist, if you wish) first forms in his mind a clear, strong, positive visualization, mental-picture, idea, or thought of what he intends the other person shall do; in this, of course, he has the benefit of long training in the practices in which you have been instructed.

2 The magician also employs "the spoken word" in the form of verbal commands (suggestions) to amplify his visualizations, and in this way accomplishes projection. That is all there is to it, but that "all" is much—for it contains the essence of East Indian Magic. Back of this straight forward procedure is found the power acquired by years of training and development along the lines of concentrate visualization, projection, and affirmation or Mantra-power.

While, naturally, the more startling phenomena along the line of this form of psychic influencing can come only after mastering the powers of the Yogi, and

Preparations for the "Pongal Festival," which is celebrated in Southern India in January. It is a three-day harvest festival. In Tamil Nadu the sun is worshipped as it moves from Cancer to Capricorn

one becomes an Adept, yet there are many wonderful manifestations of this kind possible which are elemental enough to be accomplished immediately. I will instruct you in this practice as through the mastery of such more simple phenomena, one may gradually acquire sufficient power and ability to proceed to the practice of more difficult performances.

In such practice, the first thing you should impress upon yourself is this rule: In psychic influencing, of this kind, the imagination is to be appealed to rather than the will. The will follows the imagination naturally, and does not need to be driven. The imagination may be "coaxed" or "led" gently, quietly, and subtly in the desired direction. The imagination must be allured, charmed, seduced, to accept the mental-picture that you desire to place within it, so that it will accept the same as being of its own creation.

The suggestionist might be likened to those special species of birds which lay their eggs in the nests of other birds, and make the latter hatch them. In psychic influence, you use your will, it is true, but you use it in influencing the imagination of the other person, not his will: his imagination once given the desired direction, his will, will follow that path. That is what Emile Coué, the famous French psychologist who was well known on the Continent and in America during the early part of this century, meant when he stated, "When the will and imagination are in conflict, the imagination will invariably gain the day." Coué recognized that imagination is stronger than will—this, indeed, is an age-old Yoga teaching.

The psychological effect of the environment is important in all initial experiments along the line of this form of psychic influencing. As you become a master of the art, you can be less particular about this matter. But for your first experimenting, a general atmosphere of calm and quiet, peace and harmony is helpful, and the reverse is hindering. Outside noises or sights tend to distract the mind of the "subject"—that being the name generally given to persons upon whom the psychic experiments are made. A dim light is helpful. Finally, all such experimenting must be conducted in a serious mental attitude.

The degree of "suggestibility" of various persons may be determined in advance of the formal experiments by means of a simple "test" which embodies all the essential elements and principles of the more elaborate experiments. It is an ancient Hindu test, and has proved efficacious in India for countless years of experiment and demonstration. In your beginning work in psychic influencing, you will find this test of great advantage to you as through it you will be able to eliminate lightly suggestible subjects and concentrate your attention upon the highly suggestible ones, thus obtaining striking results. This East Indian test for suggestibility is as follows:

Have the person to be tested stand in front of you, extending his left arm and hand outward from his body in a comfortable position. Have him hold his palm downward, and then raise or elevate his little finger while holding the other fingers down and steady, on a level with his palm. Then tell him that you will proceed to cause his raised finger to experience a tingling sensation, beginning at the tip of the finger, then including all the finger, and then gradually extending up his hand and arm clear to the shoulder. Tell him that the tingling sensation will be but faint at first, but will increase markedly until it becomes decidedly perceptible.

Then, while standing before him, concentrate your visualized thought on that lifted finger, "seeing and feeling" within yourself that it is actually tingling as described. As you do this, say to yourself mentally, "It is tingling, tingling, tingling. Now, it is tingling more and more all the time. He feels it now. He feels it. He feels it now." Manifest conviction and certainty in your thought, mental-picture, and verbal statement; be earnest about it as you visualize, affirm, and project the thought and visualization of the tingling into his finger. If you have practiced the Yoga methods previously given you, you will be able to do this effectively.

After a few moments of such practice, ask the subject if he can feel the tingling sensations sent to him by your thoughts, even though it be ever so faintly experienced. Be sure you ask the question in a positive way; never in the negative. For example, do not say, "Do you feel it? in a doubting, uncertain manner, as such is the negative way. Instead, confidently say, "You feel it tingling now, don't you?" That is the positive way. Emphasize the "don't" sharply and forcibly, for that word is the keynote to what is known as "a leading question," i.e., a question suggesting its own answer. There is the greatest of difference between asking questions of this kind in the negative form and in the positive one; each is a suggestion, one a negative suggestion and one a positive suggestion. Make a note of this principle as it is important to your performance of magic.

112

You will find that a decided tingling sensation is induced in many subjects in this way. Some feel a very strong tingling; others, only a faint one; and others still will feel none at all. The latter you may dismiss, telling them that they are not sufficiently sensitive to a thought impulse for successful psychic experimenting. Conversely, praise the successful ones by complimenting them on their psychic perceptive power. Always conclude the experiment by grasping the subject's hand and telling him, "The influence is all gone now; the tingling is all gone!"

By using this Hindu test, you will know immediately just how receptive or unreceptive the subjects are, and can then govern yourself accordingly. An entire roomful of persons may be tested in this manner, then selecting only the most responsive ones for further experiments. The Yogis frequently use this test in dealing with individual persons as it tells them quickly the degree of "psychic receptivity" the person possesses.

Having selected a suitable subject or subjects, using persons who have shown a good degree of suggestibility, you may proceed to conduct further experiments, graduating from the simplest on to the more complex by degrees. It is well to prepare the subject's mind in a general way for the experiments, thus securing a favorable and harmonious mental attitude on his part. Instruct him along these lines:

"Now, in these experiments, you must give me your entire attention. Clear your mind of everything else, and attend to my voice and sense my thoughts. Make yourself receptive to my words and thoughts."

Next, secure the relaxation of the subject. Request the subject to relax all the muscles of his body as much as he can. Then direct him specifically to relax his arms. Lift his hand, and let it drop back limply to his side. Suggest that he establish the idea of "limbering up" in his mind, as this physical condition is important to these experiements. Use the words "relax" and "limber" frequently in your instructions, as these have a very suggestive effect. Now gradually have the subject mentally go over the muscles of his body, i.e., the muscles of his head and face, shoulders and chest, thighs and legs. This not only serve to induce the desired physical condition for the experiments, but also puts the subject at ease mentally, and increases receptivity to your suggestions.

FIRST MAYA EXPERIMENT

This test is called "the first stage" by the Hindus. Being classified as a "posture sway experiment" it is also known to western psychologists, and demonstrated as a test in suggestion.

The test is performed by first telling the subject, now standing before you, that when he hears your words telling him to fall forward, he must then "think of falling forward," and will actually find himself slowly swaying forward, and finally falling complete forward into your arms. You promise to catch him. You may then either have him close his eyes, or else keep them open, and gaze steadily into your eyes; some subjects do better with eyes closed, while others respond best with their eyes open and fixed on yours.

113

Then, say to him, "Now keep your attention fixed on me, and let my thought flow into you. You are feeling an inclination to fall forward . . . fall forward . . . fall forward! Let yourself go and respond. I will catch you as you fall forward. Now you are coming . . . you are falling forward toward me, slowly. Now you are commencing to sway forward faster over towards me. Sway, sway, SWAY over towards me. Fall forwards NOW!"

As you give these affirmations (suggestions), make passes with your hands drawing from each side of his head towards yourself, as if actually *drawing* him to you. Throw yourself into the "drawing procedure." It increases the power of the suggestions. In a few moments, the subject will sway and fall forward, as you have willed that he should. Also, during the entire experiment visualize the subject as "falling forward," and project the thought to him of his "falling forward."

In this first experiment in elementary Maya, you will note, you are manifesting the entire process of the oriental magicians—the three phases of creative Yoga: visualization, projection and affirmation. Transplant the actors to India, furnish the necessary costumes and native audience, and you would have here a typical exhibition of the elementary methods of the Hindu wonder workers.

SECOND MAYA EXPERIMENTS

These tests produce a mental control of the muscles, and advances up the scale of psychic influence. I will give you a number of such experiments. In all of these tests remember always to hold the visualized thought represented by the suggestive words you are hurling at the subject via the visualization, projection, and affirmation method of the Yogis.

(a) Have the subject place the palm of his hand upon your palm, pressing it down firmly upon yours. Then tell him that you will fasten his palm to yours by thought-force. Say to him, "Press your palm tightly against my palm. Press tight, tight! Our two palms are becoming fastened together so tightly, you will find that you cannot take it away from mine. You can't take it away . . . you can't. It is stuck so tightly to mine you cannot pull it away no matter how hard you try. Try, try hard, you can't, you can't!"

Emphasize the word "can't" as you give these suggestions. After the subject has tried fruitlessly to pull his palm from yours, close the experiment by saying, "All right now . . . the thought-influence is all gone now. You can take your palm away from mine. Everything is all right!"

Always remove the impressions in this way, at the close of each of these experiments in initiate psychic influencing.

(b) Have the subject clasp his hands together, interlocking his fingers. Tell him to push his hands together as tightly and firmly as he possibly can. Then suggest that he cannot unclasp his hands try as hard as he will until you release him from the influence by thought. Emphasize the "you can't" suggestions as in the previous test in this grouping. The subject will be utterly unable to separate his locked hands until you remove the influence.

114

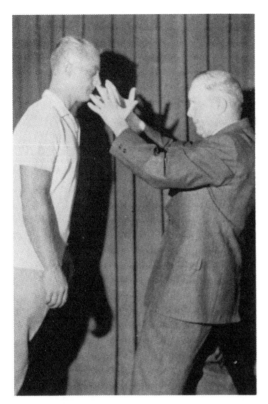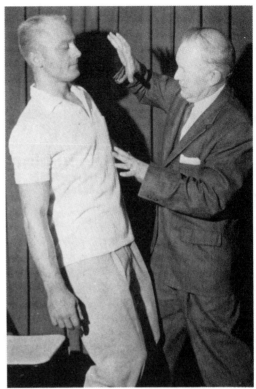

Performing preliminary experiments in Maya, oriental psychic influencing. Experiments of this type have been performed by the Initiates in India for centuries. The knowledge has infiltrated into the Occident, and such test are employed by psychologists to demonstrate "the power of suggestion."

(c) Proceeding in the same way, you may have him clench his fist tightly, and then make it impossible for him to unclench it, by the power of your concentrated-upon suggestions.

(d) You may then have him rotate his hands, around each other, telling him that he will be unable to stop rotating them until you tell him he can do so. Then give the suggestions, "That's it, faster, faster, faster; you can't stop, you can't stop, you can't stop!"

Then remove the influence as previously instructed.

(e) In the same way, the subject may be made unable to step out in a certain direction; or made unable to step over an imaginary line, or a line made by laying a piece of rope on the floor, etc.

(f) In like manner, he may be made to walk forward toward you, in obedience to the "drawing motions" of your hands; or else backward, in response to your "pushing back" passes. Or, again walk "sidewise" in response to the appropriate motions of your hands.

(g) The subject may be made to sit down in a certain chair; caused to be unable to sit down in the chair; or prevented from rising from the chair in which he is seated, in response to the magician's suggestions.

(h) The subject may be influenced so he cannot lift a light box, which you have made "as heavy as lead" by suggestion, and after you have suggested that "he cannot lift it!" Or, he may be made unable to thrown down from his hand, or to "let go" of a light cane held lengthwise in his two hands.

(i) In the same way, he may have his eylids tightly fastened, and be made unable to open them until given permission, by means of the appropriate suggestions given by you along precisely the same lines as those previously described. In all of these muscular influencing experiments, the suggestion "you can't" is the effective element. The arms, legs, etc. may also be "stiffened" and held tightly and firmly in a rigid position by the influence. And the subject's lips may be fastened together so that he cannot open his mouth and say his own name until you release him.

THIRD MAYA EXPERIMENTS

These tests advance up the scale of psychic control as you influence the senses. By the employment of the techniques you have learned, you can produce some very interesting effects in induced sensations. Experiments of this nature require a greater degree of receptivity to the suggestions. Use for these tests subjects who have proved responsive to the foregoing demonstrations; you will be able to cause the subjects to feel, taste, smell, hear, and see imaginary things, or else temporarily to have one or more of his senses inhibited. Following are a variety of such psychic influencing experiments:

(a) For causing the experiencing of a maya "burning sensation," have your subject stand before you and extend his hand, palm downward. Place the first two fingers of your right hand upon the back of his hand, concentrating your gaze upon it earnestly, and at the same time visualize and project towards his hand the thought that he is feeling the sensation of "burning" where your fingers touch his hand. At the same time in affirmation say to him, "My fingers where they touch your hand feel hot, hot, hot! You can feel them burning your hand! You feel it! It burns you! Pull your hand away!" Emphasize the words "hot" and "burning," as you give these affirmation suggestions.

A large percentage of receptive subjects will experience the sensation of "burning heat" if the thought and affirmation are made sufficiently strong and vivid. An interesting variation may be performed by giving the subject a coin to hold between his thumb and forefinger, and making it "hot, hot, burning hot" in the way just described. Again, anything can be made "freezing cold" in the same manner, by varying the thought and the affirmation suggestions. Likewise the subject may be made to feel the temperature of the room become uncomfortably warm or cold, as the case may be. Hot and cold sensation are among the most readily produced of induced sensations.

Sometimes other persons in the room observing such experiments will also "take on" the imaginary sense deception, as a sympathetic response. Cases have been known in which blisters have been produced in experiments of this nature in which a postage stamp has been affixed to the subject's body, with the thought and affirmation that it is a tiny "blistering plaster." Scientific tests have been made along these lines with startling results.

(b) In the same general way, the subject (or a roomful of responsive persons) may be made to experience the sensation of "smell"—pleasant or unpleasant, according to the thought and affirmation of the demonstrator. Hold up a perfume bottle which is filled only with plain water, but think of it strongly to yourself as being perfume, and affirm positively that you will uncork the bottle and waft it through the air, and the spectators are to tell you when they smell the pleasant fragrance. You can make the smell be violets, magnolias, orange blossoms, or whatever you wish. Many persons will state that they smell the odor of the perfume markedly. Or, artificial flowers may be given imaginary odors which subjects will experience. This is a classical experiment in suggestion (affirmation).

(c) Taste sensations can also be induced by these methods. Have the subject hold up his forefinger and concentrate upon its tip, while you affirm that when he touches it to his tongue it will taste bitter. The subject will sense a tart taste from his finger. Now tell him to look at his fingertip again, and this time you suggest that it will taste sweet like sugar. The affirmed suggestion will be experienced when he places his finger in his mouth.

(d) With very receptive subjects, you can induce imaginary sensations of sound. You may make the responsive subject hear the sound of a buzzing fly, a droning bee, or the distant cry of a child. Illusions of sight may also be induced in this way. The trained Hindu magicians are particularly adept in inducing sight sensations. Their proficiency is the result of years of practice in mastering the methods of Maya. An experiment you can try in this regard is to have the subject concentrate on the back of his hand while you trace a cross upon its surface with your finger. As you do this, concentrate strongly and see the cross in "your mind's eye," as you affirm that he will see it appear as a black cross before his eyes. Many subjects will testify that they can see the cross.

This splendid edifice in marble is the former palace of the Maharaja of Mysore. It has now been converted into a luxury hotel. It is an ideal base for visiting the nearby temples at Belur and Halebid, the Garden City of Bangalore, the great statue of Gomateshwara at Sravanbelgola, the city of Mysore, the Briandavan Gardens, and the Island Fortress of Srirangaoatna.

FOURTH MAYA EXPERIMENT

This test advances yet further up the scale of psychic control as you inhibit the senses. Particularly the sense of feeling may be readily "shut off" by the method of visualization, projection, and affirmation. "Hold the thought" of numbness over the hand of the subject and affirm repeatedly to him that his hand is becoming numb, numb, numb, and that he will feel no sensation in it at all. He will be found to experience a marked degree of local anaesthesia, and even if a needle is touched to the flesh, no sensation will be experienced. The Hindu magicians frequently demonstrate this phenomena in allowing large hat pins to be passed through their flesh, and even reclining upon a "bed of nails." These are popular demonstrations of the fakirs who have mastered these mind-control-over-body skills.

In performing all of these initial Maya experiments, always be sure to restore the normal conditions at the close of each test, which is very simply accomplished by the thought and affirmation presented as, "The influence is all gone now; you are all right, just as you were before." Also, I would advise that you do not carry any of these experiments in muscular control and sense sensation influencing to extremes. The Yogis easily control the circulation of the blood and functions of the physical organs in this way, but such undertakings are not recommended to the initiate.

As I commented earlier, experiments of type are related to what psychologist term "waking suggestion" or "waking hypnosis." It is interesting to note that these tests used by the magician initiate in learning of Maya are the same tests employed by western hypnotists to demonstrate "the power of suggestion." These tests have been performed in India for time immemorial. Truly, "Look to the East for from the East cometh light."

The major difference between the eastern and western techniques, in this regard, is that while the Hindu magician stresses all three elements of the psychic formula, western hypnotists stress only the third element, that of affirmation (suggestion). In the next chapter of this book, I will give you detailed instructions in my Occidental/Oriental method of hypnotizing which combines western techniques with the psychic processes of the Yogis. The results are true magic.

In closing these initial instructions in learning the art of Maya, I ask you to bear in mind, as has been repeatedly emphasized, that in the performance of all forms of mental magic, from the most elemental to the most advanced, there are always present the combined elements of the psychic formula, viz.: (1) visualization, or mental-picture, (2) projection of thought, or propulsive will, (3) affirmation, or verbal statement. And the effect is always produced in just the one way of action upon the imagination and through the imagination upon the will of the other person—the imagination leading the will and making the path over which the will travels.

Of such is MAYA, oriental psychic influencing.

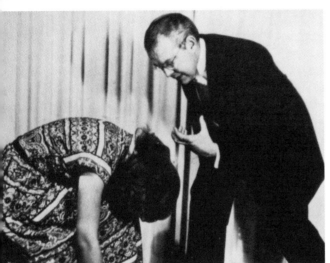

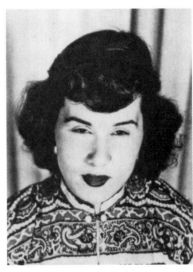

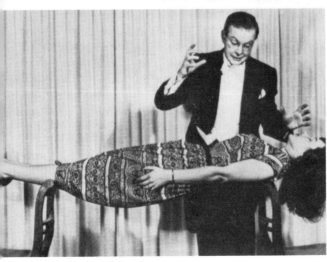

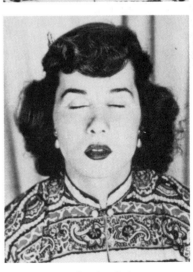

Ormond McGill performing various phases of hypnotic phenomena. In the Orient, performances of Maya are the related counterparts of Hypnotism demonstrations in the Occident, but are much advanced in psychically influencing aspects, as you will learn in these studies.

11

Occidental/Oriental Hypnotism

As a professional magician/hypnotist, I was fascinated by Maya. It will be noted in maya the psychically induced effects are produced in the awake condition of the subject's mind. Hypnosis as a condition associated with sleep seems to be entirely a product of the occident. Suggestions of sleep have for so long been used in the various western methods of inducing hypnosis that many people regard hypnosis and sleep as being almost synonymous. However, actually the states are quite different as in sleep the attention is diffused, while in hypnosis the attention is keenly activated. And attention is a characteristic of wakefulness. Modern psychological studies now consider hypnosis as being more close allied to wakefulness than it is to sleep, an observation the Yogis have long known, as evidenced by their methods of maya.

However, hypnosis should in no sense be regarded as a condition of normal consciousness (wakefulness). The mental condition known as hypnosis is distinctly a unique state of mind of itself. While the state retains the elements of consciousness (as opposed to the unconsciousness of sleep), it is a state of mind produced by a transference to another level of consciousness. A state with capacities of mental activities distinctly its own that are directly keyed to the sympathetic nervous system rather than being keyed to the central nervous system, as in the case of our more familiar everyday mental processes operating in normal consciousness. As such is it related to the maya of the Yogis.

While in India, I began designing my own method of hypnotizing using the Yogi techniques combined with those of occidental processes. The method I finally designed is the one which I will give you in this chapter; it is the culmination of some years of experimenting.

I have named this method by the descriptive one of Occidental/Oriental Hypnotism, since it effectively embodies the ancient process of the maya of the Orient along with suggestive techniques (including suggestions of "sleep,"

120

which have for so long been associated with hypnosis as to have become an integral part of it) of the Occident. As a result of my experimenting, I have found this to be an effective method of hypnotizing many subjects who are resistant to other techniques; a method designed directly for the positive induction of deep hypnosis for the purpose of hypnotic experimenting and psychical development.

As a student of East Indian Magic, you should have this knowledge.

These instructions cover every detail of the procedure so that nothing is left to guesswork, and the method can be immediately applied with extremely effective results. In the study, I will likewise resume the basic principles of maya for your comprehensive study of oriental hypnotism as they apply specifically to this hypnotic technique.

Utilizing many unique subtleties as this method does, the student who is interested in hypnotism is urged to follow the modus operandi with exactitude, as it offers much to the art/science of hypnotism, as a contribution from the real magic of India.

In the Orient, the Adept regard the induction of hypnosis to be greatly affected by his own mental attitude as a mind-influence over his subject. As you have learned, according to oriental belief there are three basic principles of psychic influencing: Visualization, Projection, and Affirmation. In the production of deep hypnosis in subjects by this East Indian method, these principles must be kept constantly in mind, and are to be applied throughout the entire process, viz.:

In presenting the suggestions and/or "sleep formula," you, as the hypnotizer, must constantly visualize the expected results of the suggestions you present as occurring. This means that you must form and hold firmly in your mind the mental-picture of how the subject will be in reality after he or she responds to your affirmations (suggestions). In other words, see "in your mind's eye" your subject in precisely the condition you suggest, in responding to each suggestion.

Next project your visualized mental-picturing to be fact into the mind of your subject both through the positive assurance of your affirmative verbal suggestions, and the direct psychic influence of your thoughts.

And throughout the entire process, affirm positively through your voice, your speech, your gestures and every effort that the visualized and projected state you have created in your mind will become an actuality in the subject.

It is in this combining of techniques that the great difference between Oriental Hypnotism and western methods occur, for the latter makes use of only the indirect influence over the mind of the subject produced by verbal suggestions, while the former uses not only this important medium but combines it with the direct influence over the mind by the power of visualized thought and projected will. As Adepts explain it, it is the power of these two forces working together as a unit that accounts for the remarkable results attributed to Oriental Hypnotism which outshine the best of occidental phenomena.

And so the Adepts emphasize, in applying this oriental method, use the inner powers of your mind when you hypnotize. Visualize strongly exactly the state you wish created in the subject, project this mental-picture with your will, and affirm with positive conviction that the image will become a reality. Knowing that which is to occur shall occur by both firm conviction in your suggestion formula (verbalized thoughts) and the direct thought projection through your concentration on the desired results.

The above is your pattern for the process of successfully hypnotizing by the oriental method. And remember, by strong direct thought projection through concentration on the desired results, it is not meant that you must strain in your mental efforts to push your thoughts out to your subject. Such is entirely an erroneous impression of what is meant by projection. In actuality, the process is very easy and natural; it being merely necessary to form the mental-picture in your mind (and the more clearly and sharply you form it the better), and then extend your visualization to include in "the mind picture" the impression that it is passing out from you and is draping about the subject to encompass him in a sort of "mental mold," as it were, to which his response will be to conform as you mentally visualize. The process once mastered is readily performed, it does not require any mental strain whatsoever, and your visualized thoughts will automatically flow to your subject as you hypnotize following these directions.

Even judged entirely by western understanding of psychology, there is much to recommend this procedure, for to make suggestions effective they must be given with positive assurance, and how better to secure such firm conviction in the presentation of the suggestions than by this deliberate process of concentration on the thoughts behind the words, and the direct attempt to project those thoughts outward to influence the mind of the subject.

We come now to one further point in the directions of the Eastern Adepts for Oriental Hypnotism, and that is to charge your visualized projected thoughts with Prana.

As you have learned, prana is regarded as a form of psychical energy of universal presence that can be used by the Adept to energize his psychic efforts. You use it in precisely this way in the present instance of visualization, projection, and affirmation in relation to this hypnotic process. As access to prana is effectively generated by rhythmic breathing, in this connection you will now be given a simple means of charging both yourself and your subject with prana.

As occidental procedure of hypnosis recognizes a dynamic condition of cooperation between the hypnotist and the subject, it will be found good procedure to commence this cooperation on a mutual effort right during the interview portion of the induction. By having your subject engage in the prana charging exercise with you, you accomplish thus a dual purpose:

1 Keying up of both your own powers and the sensitivity of your subject by the prana charging process.

2 Producing a strong psychological bound of cooperation between yourself and your subject in the mutual performance of an activity.

Both of the above objectives are important to deep hypnotic induction by this oriental method.

The understanding being now complete as to what is to be your mental attitude maintained through the entire hypnotization by this method of OCCIDENTAL/ORIENTAL HYPNOTISM, I shall proceed on to the step-by-

The Interview. Fig. 1.

step details of the hypnotic induction technique, using these combination of procedures. First we will study the interview.

Seating yourself opposite the person who has volunteered to be hypnotized, explain to him (or her) that the process of being hypnotized is not to be regarded as mysterious, that any intelligent person can easily enter hypnosis. The experience is relaxing and refreshing just like normally going to sleep is, as they do every night of this life. Only in this case they place themselves into the special condition of hypnosis, by deliberate suggestions of relaxation and sleep, rather than by the spontaneous process of going to bed. See Fig. 1.

Having established the naturalness of the experience the person is attempting, go on to explain that since the method of hypnotic induction you will be using is Oriental in nature, you are going to ask the person to indulge in a special breathing exercise prior to your hypnotizing him.

Have your subject perform the following exercise right along with you. (You will note that in this you are performing the rhythmic breathing method which you have previously studied in Chapter four of this book.)

Sit upright in your chair, place your feet flat on the floor, with your spine straight. Your subject performs all actions right along with you. Count slowly to establish a rhythm rate, from one to six. Together, now, with your subject inhale for the count of six (count mentally as you have established together the rate of your counting—1, 2, 3, 4, 5, 6). Hold the breath for the count of 1, 2, 3. Exhale slowly following this same rhythmic count from one to six—1, 2, 3, 4, 5, 6. Perform this breathing exercise seven times together.

At this point, explain to your subject that while he performs the next phase of this initial breathing exercise he is to think passively of letting himself become drowsy and going to sleep. You, in turn, concentrate your thoughts on becoming charged with pranic energy which will make your thoughts powerful in influencing your subject as you visualize, project, and affirm.

123

Yoga has gone modern in some parts of India. Here in the Kovalam Grove Beach Resort in Kerala, popular forms of yoga are taught to students who come from many different countries.

Now, have your subject place his finger to his nose and stop off the air passage in his left nostril; while you, in like manner, place your finger to your nose and stop off the air passage in your right nostril. Restricting your breathing thus, perform together again the rhythmic breathing exercise. Perform this exercise seven times together in unison. This handling is correct for the effective performance of maya, and establishes a rapport between you and your subject.

Request your subject to now relax, and ask him to recall a time when he was tired and dozed off to sleep in a chair or on a couch. Explain that this experience of being hypnotized will feel exactly like that; all he is going to do, as far as experience goes, is simply dozing off to sleep; the difference being that when he dozed off before he was physically tired, while, in this instance, you will make him feel tired by having him concentrate on ideas of tiredness and sleepiness until he gently dozes off to sleep in his chair.

This handling of the interview is highly significant: (1) It removes fear from the hypnotizing experience and associates it with a familiar process (that of naturally going to sleep). (2) It has engaged both you and your subject in a mutual process of activity. (3) It has charged both of you with positive and negative prana as used in maya, and has developed a rapport between you in the mutual performing of the oriental breathing exercises. Both of you, in your respective roles of subject and hypnotist, are now ready to proceed on with the hypnotizing process.

Ask your subject to sit back comfortably in his chair, place his feet flat on

124

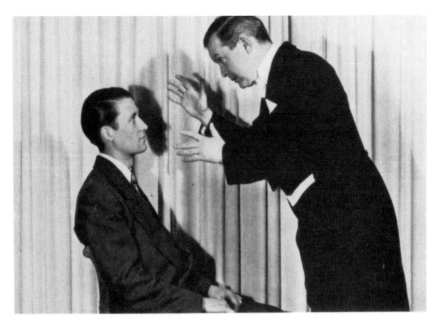

The Induction of Hypnosis. Fig. 2.

the floor, rest his hands on his knees so his fingers do not touch each other, and to concentrate his entire attention on your eyes.

You stand directly before your subject and gaze upon his eyes. Rather than looking directly at his eyes, gaze through him by focusing your eyes on an imaginary point about five feet in back of his head. You will find this hypnotic gazing technique very compelling in holding the subject's attention, and yet it is not fatiguing to your eyes.

Having directed the subject's attention, commence your flow of affirmation suggestions, and, as you talk, make gentle passes downward in the direction of your subject. Perform these in a sort of elipse, starting with both hands near your face, then bringing them out and downward toward the subject; completing the elongated circle by bringing your hands back again towards your face. Make these passes unobtrusive; more to emphasize the subject's attention to your eyes and suggestions than to cause notice of themselves.

See Fig. 2 for position, gaze, and hypnotic pass details.

Right from this very starting point in the hypnotizing process, commence your oriental techniques of visualizing, projection, and affirmation. As you present the following suggestions and perform the various manipulations, visualize in "your mind's eye" the response to be such as you desire it to occur, and project that mental-picture to the subject along with the suggestions you are giving him. Let your suggestions serve as the affirmation of what you see occurring via your visualizing and projection. This is the Oriental approach to hypnotizing, and will make all the difference in the world in the striking and deeply moving hypnotic effects you will produce on your subjects.

With this understanding of your inner processes of mind that you carry out simultaneously with your outward processes, give the following suggestions while visualizing strongly precisely the effects your words are designed to develop. Suggest:

"Relax back in your chair, let every muscle of your body be completely at rest, and keep your attention concentrated on my eyes . . . and forget everything else, except your one desire to go to sleep. Everything is beginning to feel so very, very comfortable. It just seems so good to thus relax and let everything go. Your whole body seems so warm and comfortable . . . and as the pleasant warmth begins to penetrate through every muscle of your body, you are relaxing more and more comfortably and pleasantly in your chair. Everything is so very pleasant, comfortable, and warm."

Notice how the affirmation suggestions up to this point concentrate entirely on bodily comfort, relaxation, and pleasant repose.

"Now, as you relax back in your chair, your gaze is becoming more and more concentrated on my eyes, and your eyes are beginning to become very, very heavy and tired. It is hard to keep your eyelids open; they are so very, very, heavy and tired . . . but they won't close yet because you are concentrating so forcefully upon my eyes. But, now, as I count slowly from one to ten, your eyes will begin to close. Close your eyelids anytime you wish as I count slowly from one to ten, shutting out the light. One . . . Two. How very heavy and tired your eyes are. How they burn. How you want to close them. They are so tired. Three. Close them now, shutting out the light. Four. Your eyelids feel like lead. Close them tight now shutting out the light, let them rest. Five. Six. Your eyes are closing right down tightly together. Close them tight. That's it. Eyes all closed right down together. Seven. Eyes all closed shutting out the light. Eyelids closed tight together. Eight. It feels so good to just close those tired, tired eyes, and let everything be quiet and dark. Nine, TEN! Eyes all closed tight together now, everything is all quiet and dark."

Notice how the affirmation suggestions in this section of "The Sleep Formula" concentrate entirely on the closing of the eyelids. Visualize and project the thought of the eyelids closing tightly. Most subjects will have their eyes closed by the time you reach the count of "five," and almost invariably by the time you reach the count of "ten." Should it ever happen that your subject does not have his eyes closed by the last count, lean forward, and, with your fingertips, gently close them.

The suggestions continue:

"Eyes all closed in darkness now. Now, go to sleep. Go deep to sleep. Everything is gently drifting and floating gently by . . . and you are sinking down, down, down deep to sleep. Just floating and drifting gently as though on a cloud . . . and you are sinking on down, down, down, to sleep. Go to sleep! Go deep, deep to sleep. How tired you are. Every muscle in your body just calls for sleep . . . wonderful, restful sleep that will take away every tiredness. How tired you are, so tired, so very tired. You need to sleep . . . wonderful restful sleep. So go to sleep! Go fast, fast to sleep! You can feel that wonderful rest and relaxation creeping through your entire body, and you are drifting . . . drifting . . . drifting and floating on down, down to deep, sound, wonderful sleep. Everything is just fading, fading, fading, fading far, far away . . . down into deep, wonderful, peaceful sleep."

126

Notice how the affirmation suggestions in this phase of the induction concentrate on release from all tiredness, and the peace and rest that can be found in sleep. As you give these suggestions, mentally-picture your subject as being in this condition. Now, comes a very important bit of technique: standing at the side of your subject, whisper your suggestions directly into his ear, and as you do this concentrate on a flow of prana in your breath passing into his being along with your affirmations. See fig. 3.

"Go deep asleep now! That's it, go deep asleep! Sound, sound asleep! You are sinking on down and down into a deep, sound sleep. Go deep asleep now! Go sound asleep! You are breathing deep and free. Breath deep and free. Your breaths are coming in deeper and deeper, and every breath you take is sending you on down deeper and deeper to sleep."

Watch your subject carefully at this point. If his breathing begins to deepen in response to your suggestions, you can begin to gauge the depth of trance that is commencing to develop. Stand up now, and speak while standing behind your subject:

"Nothing can disturb you. All is so quiet and calm. Breathe deeply, and go deeply to sleep. Your muscles are all so very relaxed that your head is beginning to get very, very heavy . . . so heavy is it nodding forward onto your chest. Your head is nodding forward . . . it is falling forward onto your chest."

Watch your subject's head; if it nods and falls limply forward onto his chest, proceed right on . . . otherwise, continue longer with your affirmations of sleep and relaxation, and gently push his head forward onto his chest. Then place your hands, one on each of his shoulders, at the sides of the neck, and push down firmly so his body tends to slump into the chair. See fig. 4.

Next exert pressure, with your right forefinger, between the top two vertebra; these are easily located as they stand out prominently due to the bent forward position of the neck. See fig. 5.

As you press in firmly on this spot, forcefully suggest, "Go to sleep now, fast, fast to sleep!" Next, place the tip of your right forefinger directly on the bridge of the entranced subject's nose and press in firmly, and continue to suggest forcefully, "Go to sleep! Go deep, deep to sleep!" See fig. 6.

Then take the subject's hand in yours and press firmly on the base of the nails of the first two fingers, and forcefully suggest, "Sleep! Go deep, deep to sleep." See fig. 7. In this technique you are making use of pressure upon what are called "The Hypnogenic Zones," and the affirmation suggestions given at this time should be commanding and forceful. You are ready now to apply a very effective procedure that will deepen the hypnosis. Suggest:

"Your jaw is slackening now. The muscles of your face and jaw are relaxing completely. Open your mouth just a bit. That's it. Open your mouth . . . just a bit."

As you give these suggestions, run your fingers gently down each side of the subject's jaw, and continue your affirm ion until you get the desired response, and his jaw hangs open. See fig. 8.

Suggest: "Keep your mouth gently open now, and inhale very slowly a deep, deep breath. Inhale now . . . that's it . . . a deep, deep breath. Hold it. Hold it! Slowly, slowly exhale now. That's it. Exhale! And again now, inhale

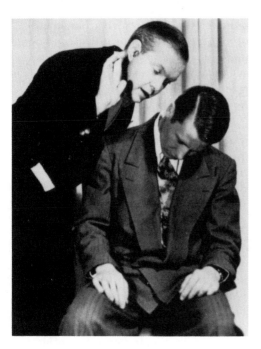

Fig. 3.

Fig. 4.

Fig. 5.

Fig. 6.

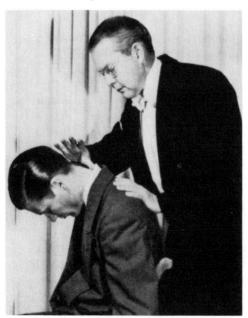

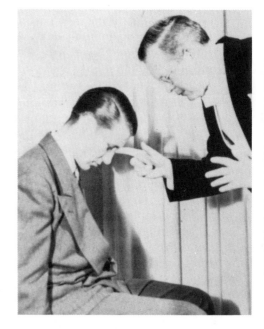

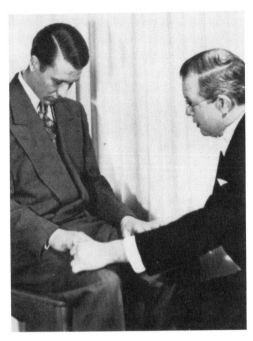

Fig. 7.

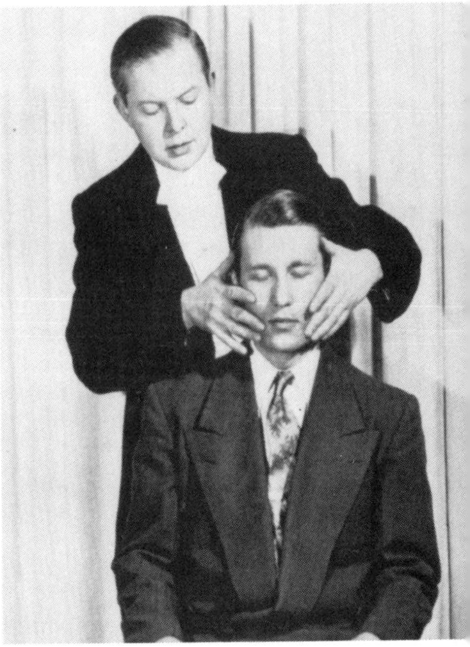

Fig. 8.

Fig. 9.

Fig. 10.

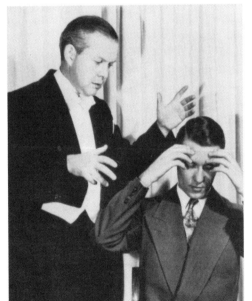

129

very slowly. Inhale slowly. Inhale very slowly. How sleepy you are becoming. How very, very sleepy. Go deep, deep to sleep. All right now, inhale again; inhale deep. Hold it, and now exhale very slowly. Exhale very, very slowly . . . and go deep, deep to sleep. Inhale . . . that's it . . . exhale . . . inhale . . . exhale . . . and go deep, deep to sleep. And again, inhale deep, deep, very deep . . . hold it, and go to sleep as you exhale so very, very slowly. Go deep, deep, deep asleep."

You have employed a technique here that is physically sleep inducing, and combined with your psychical processes and suggestions is virtually irresistable. Stop your commands of deliberate inhaling and exhaling at this point, and watch your subject closely. In many cases the deep breathing once started will continue on automatically.

"Sleep deep now. Wonderful restful sleep is all that matters. Nothing can disturb you or bother you. Nothing can awaken you. Every breath you take is sending you on down deeper and deeper to sleep. Breathe deep and free, and go deep, deep to sleep."

Notice that emphasis at this stage of the induction has been concentrated on the breath control of the subject. Your subject, at this point, should be thoroughly relaxed, slumped down in his chair with head resting limply on chest, and his breathing coming in slow and deep—to every appearance deep asleep. You are ready now to begin some physical stimuli and muscular responses.

"A warm sensation is coming into your body, and you can feel a tingling in your fingertips. A tingling exactly like the nerves feel when they go to sleep. That tingling is becoming very strong. (Visualize and project strongly these sensations to your subject as you give these suggestions.) Now, it is passing up from your fingers over your hands, and on up your arms, and you are going deeper and deeper to sleep. Go deep, deep to sleep! Now your fingers, on your

Fig. 11.   Fig. 12.

 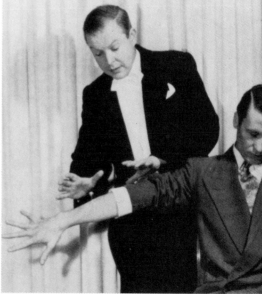

The Island Palace of Udaipur. This magnificent palace of white and pale sandstone rises out of the still, reflecting waters of the lakes of Udaipur. Udaipur is known as the city of lakes and palaces. This is a sixth-century bastioned city named after its founder, Maharaja Udai Singh. The palace with its tile and mirror inlays, mosaics of peacocks and princes, is poised over Lake Pitchola.

lap, are becoming very restless. It is hard to keep them still, they are getting so restless, they want to move up from your lap. Your hands are becoming very light . . . they are lifting right up from your lap into the air. Raise your hands right up from your lap into the air. Raise them up. That's it. The muscles of your arms are automatically pulling them up. Up! Up! Right up from your lap into the air. Now, your hands are moving up to touch your forehead. Touch your forehead with your hands. And when your hands touch your forehead, everything will disappear in blackness, everything will fade away, and you will be sound, sound asleep. Sound asleep. Touch your forehead now with your hands and sleep . . . sleep in deep sound sleep."

Notice in this phase of the induction you are testing for a direct hypnotic response, and the quality of same will indicate the depth of trance you have produced so far. Whatever the response, keep your suggestions continuous until the subject's hands leave his lap, rise up through the air, and eventually reach his forehead. You have an important bit of technique here that bridges the boundry between the conscious and subconscious threshold of complete hypnosis in what is termed "Compounded Suggestion"—the response to one suggestion setting off the response to another.

Remember to always force these movement responses. If your subject resists movement of his hands and arms as you command, then gently lift his hands up and get them started in their movements. On releasing the hands, they will then continue on of their own volition. Here is a vital secret in hypnotizing difficult subjects, i.e. when they do not respond automatically to your suggestions, then you must forcefully train them in the art of being a somnambulist.

131

Once you have your subject's hands touching his forehead as in Fig. 9, suggest:

"Sleep deeply now, and when I say 'three,' your hands will fall limp as rags to your side, and you will be fast, fast asleep. One, two, three."

You are "compounding suggestions." Also, this provides you with another indicator of your subject's depth of trance. If his responses are positive and immediate, you can proceed rapidly on. If slow, uncertain, or sluggish, then retard your technique and continue with repetitions of the suggestions you have employed up to this point. Always build towards quick, spontaneous, and automatic responses to your hynotic commands.

Next, take the subject's right hand in yours, and start moving it around in a large circle. With every revolution suggest:

"You are going deeper and deeper to sleep. You are deep, deep asleep. You are fast, fast asleep. Deep, deep asleep. Fast, fast asleep. Deep, deep, asleep. Fast, fast asleep. You are deep, deep asleep."

Let loose of his arm now, and it will continue revolving of its own volition. You can use this revolving arm indicator to judge how best to present suggestion affirmations to your subject, viz., if when you release his arm it continues revolving around and around by itself, you can feel assured that you have induced deep hypnosis, and are working with a spontaneous type of subject from whom you can secure hypnotic responses with very brief commands. If the subject's arm continues on revolving as the result of your verbal command to that effect, it is indicative that this subject is best handled through repetition and understanding of all commands. If the subject still does not respond, it indicates that you are working with either a lethargic type of person, or that the hypnosis is not yet deeply enough established for the following of hypnotic commands—in which case, continue with your hypnotic sleep developing suggestions until you obtain the desired reactions. See fig. 10. Follow on with your suggestions:

"Your arm is revolving around and around by itself . . . nothing can stop it, and you are deep, deep asleep. Your arm is beginning to get heavy now; it is falling to your side, and when it touches your side, you will become more deeply asleep than ever. Your arm is falling now, falling, falling down to your size, limp as a rag. You are completely relaxed and deep, deep asleep."

The subject's arm will fall limply to his side almost at once. Stand behind the subject now, and start revolving his head around and around: First over to the right side, then on around to the front, the left side, back, right side again, and so on. See fig. 11. Continue on moving it around and around and around, and then gently remove your hands and it will continue on its circular motions of its own volition. Let the head revolve for a few moments, and then suggest:

"Sleep, sleep deep now. Sleep deep and sound in a complete and dreamless sleep. You will follow perfectly every suggestion I present to you. Sleep deep now! Your head is stopping its rotations and is coming to rest comfortably on your chest. Sleep deep now, and follow perfectly my every suggestion."

Take your subject's arm and hold it outstretched as you command that it is stiff in that position and can not be bent. See fig. 12. All of the subject's efforts to move his arm will prove in vain. Command the arm to drop, and it instantly falls to his side. Your subject is now deeply entranced in the somnambulistic condition of hypnosis, and will promptly follow your hypnotic commands. Strive now to deepen this somnambulistic state by directly developing a sensory response. Suggest:

"It is beginning to become very warm in this room. It is getting so very, vary warm that you are becoming positively hot in this room; it is so warm and so hot that you are very uncomfortable. Wipe away the perspiration from your forehead; wipe away the perspiration and relieve the heat. (Carefully watch your subject's responses. Continuously barrage with repetition of your suggestions and get the subject to react as spontaneously as possible.) It is so hot in that chair that you want to stand up from it and get cool. Stand up and get cool. (When you have the subject standing, suggest:) Ah, it is so nice and cool now that you are standing. All is nice and cool. All the heat is gone now, and you are sleeping deeply and comfortably. Your body is going limp and you are falling back into your chair fast asleep." (Grip your subject by the shoulders as you give these suggestions, and ease him back into his chair.)

Notice how, step by step, you have gauged your hypnotic induction technique until its culmination results in complete hypnosis. This principle of training the subject in the art of being a somnambulist is an innovation in obtaining hypnotic results.

Having hypnotized your subject, remember these four important procedures to assure continued perfect results:

1   Between each test with the subject, continue to give suggestions that he is sleeping deeply, and that every breath he takes is sending him

The beautiful "Garden of Fountains and Flowers," which was designed originally by the third Mughal Emperor, Jehangir, for his beloved queen, Nur Jehan, is the scene for this twentieth-century seasonal spectacular. Electronically synchronized light, sound, music, and fountains blend together to bring to life bygone days of Mughal splendor and romance in the famed "Bara Dari."

133

continuously on down deeper and deeper to sleep. (Breathing being a continuous process, this associating the deeping of sleep with breathing provides a powerful factor in "setting" the trance.) Such repetition of suggestions will keep the subject from slipping out of the trance, as sometimes occurs as the result of body movements.

2   Only present one suggested response at a time, allow its complete establishment, and then remove the suggestion before giving another command. By such technique you can avoid all possible complications that sometimes arise from conflicting suggestions.

3   In giving suggestions to the hypnotized subject, present them in a positive and commanding fashion: make your commands direct and to the point.

4   Before removing the subject from the hypnotic state, give these suggestions:

"Remember, the next time you try hypnotism with me and look into my eyes, you will at once become very sleepy, your eyes will close, and you will go immediately deep to sleep in the hypnotic trance. Remember, when you look into my eyes you will go immediately fast to sleep in hypnosis."

These suggestions produce a posthypnotic effect, and "condition" the subject's return to the hypnotic state whenever that person works with you. Such handling will produce rapid rehypnotizations in subsequent sessions with that particular subject.

Having hypnotized your subject, you are now ready to remove the trance, and "awaken" the subject. Continue your suggestions as follows:

"You are fast asleep now. It has been a most wonderful, restful, and healthful sleep. And when I awaken you, in just a few moments, you will awaken feeling fine and well. I will count from one to five, and with every count you will slowly awaken, and, by the time I reach the count of 'five,' you will be wide awake! And you will awaken exactly as you do every morning of your life after a night of sound, dreamless sleep. You will feel fine and refreshed; all has been a pleasant, dreamless sleep. You will have no memory of anything; it has all been just a pleasant, dreamless sleep. You will feel fine and refreshed after this night's sleep of dreamless slumber. Remember, you will awaken exactly the same as you do every morning of your life after a night of deep, healthful sleep. And you will awaken without memory of anything whatsoever; when you awaken, it will seem exactly as thought you have merely closed your eyes, dozed off to sleep, and then awoke feeling refreshed, wonderful and well."

Deep hypnosis often produces amnesia on awakening, and to get amnesia in the subject, suggest it! Forcefully affirm and insist that the subject will not remember anything, whatsoever, on awakening. Don't pull your punches in giving suggestions—always forcefully suggest the results you desire to occur, as you visualize and project your mental-picturing of the occurrences in conjunction with your affirmations.

"All ready now, it is almost time to begin thinking about getting up, but you are sleeping so deeply and comfortably it is difficult to even think of the idea that you will soon have to wake up from this deep, wonderful sleep. But it is morning now, so you must soon wake up. I am counting now. One! You are beginning to wake up. Two! Like a dream the curtain of sleep begins to lift.

134

Sleep is slipping and fading away, and you are beginning to wake up. Wake up. Three! It is morning. What a wonderful night of sleep you have enjoyed. Wake up. Four! Wide awake now. Five! Wide, wide awake. That's it. Wide awake now and you just feel fine!"

This is unquestionably one of the most important developments yet designed for the removal of hypnosis. Note how the suggestions associate the awakening from the hypnotic sleep with the awakening from normal sleep. It not only awakens the subject gently and pleasantly, but the technique actually deepens the hypnosis during the awakening process—which invariably tends towards complete amnesia.

Having awakened your subject, immediately, before the person is even fully aware that they are awake, request them to again stare in your eyes, and repeat the hypnotizing process. Rehypnotize your subject by exactly the same method you employed in the first induction, but this time you will find results will occur much more rapidly, so you can proceed accordingly.

This is an important point in the training of a somnambulist. To awaken your subject, and then let him rationalize about his hypnotic experiences, removes much of the somnambulistic training you have developed so far. There is a pyramiding effect in rehypnotizations, and by plunging your subject into rehypnosis, you deepen greatly his hypnotic responsiveness.

Having deeply rehypnotized your subject, give these suggestions prior to his second awakening:

"Remember, when you wake up you will have no memory of any kind, you have merely dozed off to sleep in your chair, but when you awake you will see a chair in front of you, and you will immediately walk over to that chair and sit down in it, and then you will go instantly fast to sleep in that chair." (Repeat the foregoing suggestions three times so they are firmly "set" in the subject's mind, and then awaken your subject, as you have previously been instructed.)

Posthypnotically following the response to your suggestions, he subject will leave his chair, walk over to the other, seat himself, and will return to sleep in hypnosis. Now standing beside him, forcefully command:

"You are sleeping deeply now . . . and, remember, from this time on, whenever I snap my fingers in front of your face, as you stare into my eyes, you will go instantly to sleep. Remember, no matter what you are doing, whenever you look into my eyes, and I snap my fingers in front of your face, you will go instantly fast to sleep."

Quickly awaken the subject. Let him rest a few moments, then suddenly stare into his eyes and snap your fingers in front of his face. Instantly he will drop off to sleep in hypnosis, and you have thus "conditioned" him to become hypnotized on cue of the snapping of your fingers.

Having so put him into trance by this instantaneous method, awaken the subject and try it again; immediately he reenters hypnosis, and you have a trained somnambulist—the ultimate aim of all hypnotic techniques.

I have placed before you my method of Occidental/Oriental Hypnotism in depth, so you can use it. Master hypnotism; it is important to your mastery of the real magic of India. We will not study Advanced Maya, silent psychic influencing.

135

12
Silent Psychic Influence

In learning of Maya, you have learned of the threefold formula of Yogi psychic influence, viz., visualization, projection, and affirmation. You also know how to use it in relation to suggestion and hypnosis. This is the first state of training. When the initiate has mastered this stage, he is promoted to more advanced aspects of the subject, which is referred to as "silent psychic influence."

In this state of magical influencing, the formula of visualization, projection, and affirmation is applied in the same general way, but with an importanct major difference. In silent psychic influence the affirmation and the accompanying projection of the visualized thought are performed silently and inaudibly without the actual knowledge of the other person. It is this practice of Advanced Maya that the Hindu hypnotists have made a breakthrough from western methods as the hypnotic effects of suggestions are produced without the need for hypnosis; indeed, sometimes without the subject's awareness.

While this form of psychic influence is more difficult of performance than the verbalized affirmation techniques, and proficiency in its manifestation requires careful development by the initiate, once proficiency in advanced

maya is attained, you will find it far more effective than are the elementary forms of the phenomena. As you discovered that the "unspoken mantram" was the most powerful, the same rule applies to silent Maya.

In the phenomena of silent psychic influence, the chitta is aroused and the vrittis created on its surface, in the same way as in the elemental stages of the phenomena, but in this instance no audible words are used to serve as the pattern for the vrittis reproducing the thought and mental-image in the mind of the subject or subjects. Instead, what the Yogis term a "thought form present and active" is projected from the mind of the magician and sets up a mental pattern or mold in the mind of the recipient.

This "thought form" is created by thought in the akasha, and powerfully energized with prana manifests an intense degree of vibratory motion. Coming in contact with the chitta, or "mind stuff" of the other person or persons, it imposes upon it its distinct character and rate of psychic vibration, and thus sets up vritti waves in the chitta of the person, or, in other words, it reproduces in his mind the thought projected to him.

You will observe at once that this involves the principle that thought may be transmitted over space, just as speech and sight may be via radio waves. Western knowledge has been slow to recognize this principle which has long been regarded as a fundamental fact taught in oriental psychology. To the people of India, the fact that thought "travels" is no more strange or wonderful than the fact that light or heat travels in space.

This thought projection in silent psychic influence, however, is different from ordinary thought transference, as the latter usually requires a specific rapport between persons. In silent psychic influence there is no such attunement, and it is not mere thoughts which are projected but rather a "thought form" along a psychic path through space which is physically set up between the projector and the recipient. In this there is not merely a "wave" or energy charged with thought; instead there is an astral or etheric "form" charged with prana which travels unerroringly to its mark.

In the preformance of this manifestation, the magician "sees" in his mind that the pathway is established and "wills" that it be kept open for the passage of the thought-form. When the latter is created by visualization, it is projected by the will of the magician, after having charged with prana by means of thought and will. In this description of the modus operandi it sounds complicated, but it is really quite simple and easily performed once the "knack" has been acquired. I will give you full directions for the technique.

As this performance of advanced maya is important to the magician, I asked Sadhu Parimal Bandhu to expound further on the matter. He commented, "When we say that 'thoughts are things,' we are not merely using this phrase in a figurative sense; we are expressing a literal truth. We mean that thought is as much a 'thing' as is light, heat, electricity, or other forms of manifestations of nature. It is a tenuous thing yet decidedly real. And it has power, just as these others forces in nature, which I have mentioned, have power. When thought is sent forth with strength, it usually carries with it a certain amount of prana, which gives it additional power, often producing startling effects. The prana actually 'vitalizes' the thought in some cases, and makes of it almost a living force."

At the Temple of the Higher Magic, Delhi, India, these huge scientific/magical instruments are made of stone.

The effects of silent psychic influence may be produced upon persons with whom one is in immediate personal contact, and also upon persons who are at a distance. The principles employed are the same in both cases, and distance in space does not render the process more difficult. Indeed, those proficient in these methods hold that the impersonal manifesation of this power over distance is frequently easier to achieve than when the other person is in direct contact. In other words, one might say that "the invisible process" is frequently more effective than is "the visible process."

In the performance of silent psychic influence, the magician holds a clear and definite mental-picture of the person and what is desired to be accomplished by the setting up in one's own chitta, or "mind stuff," the exact pattern that is desired to occur in the chitta of the other persons. The Yogis more successful will be the manifestation. The process is explained as being accomplished by the setting up in one's own Chitta, or "mind stuff," the exact pattern that is desired to occur in the Chitta of the other persons. The Yogis instruct the initiate to "see," "feel," and "will" the desired response from the other person; the mental attitude being of absolute assurance in "knowing" that the silent commands will be followed without question. Performed in this manner, silent psychic influence is most effective.

Conversely, if the mental-image is weak in the magician's chitta, its effects will be weak in the chitta of the recipient. Now here is an important point to keep in mind, the operation of silent psychic influence is much like the process of electrical induction. What occurs in one field is transferred to the other, and in this regard it is important that you know exactly what you want before you can cause the other person to carry out that which you desire. To this end, before you attempt silent psychic influencing, you must create in your own mind a positive ideal which you wish to have reproduced in the mind of the other person or persons.

The first law then of influencing others by the silent psychic method is to have the whole thing clearly "mapped out" in your own mind: know clearly, definitely, and postively exactly what you want him to do, say, or think; just when he is to do this; just how he is to do it. Your psychic process in silent influencing is much like a stage director who moves the actors about the stage in accordance to the script which he has studied in advance.

I can effectively bring the process home to you best by removing it completely, for the moment, from the realm of magic and taking it into the field of practical, everyday business relationships. In this field, the power can be used to bring remarkable success.

In relation to business, think first in terms of the interview that is going to occur when you meet the person or prospect for whatever the purpose may be. In advance, go over in your imagination and "see the interview" exactly as you wish it to occur, with the person you are contacting as responding precisely as you wish him to. Mental-picture the interview situation and project it towards the person you are to meet. Accordingly, get the whole proceeding mapped out, charted, pictured—visualized—in your mind before the time of the interview.

This is literally lifting a page from the scroll of the successful Hindu

Not far distant from the Temple of Meenakshi in Madurai is this three-hundred-square-mile sanctuary for India's wildlife. It is built around an artificial lake. Here on these plains of Thekkady and Periyar may frequently be seen the wild elephants of India.

Located in Madurai some 489 kilometers from Madras in Southern India, the Menakshi Temple with its massive gopurams (towers) depicting hundreds of figures of Hindu dieties, is one of the most important centers of East Indian pilgrimages. A highlight of the temple is its hall of a thousand pillars, and worshippers bathe in "The Golden Lily" tank before entering the temple, which is dedicated to Menakshi, the spouse of Lord Shiva.

magician who mentally "presets" his show of maya in advance of its performance.

Let us follow on now to what may be called a psychic "preparatory treatment" of the mind of the other person in relation to a business interview. In this, you visualize exactly how you wish it to occur; you will prepare the soil of the mind of the other person for the thought-seeds which you will sow into it when you meet him. Or, to express it another way, you create a "mental path" over which his thoughts and will may easily travel at the time of the interview. Many of the most successful business men have picked up this ancient oriental secret and have adopted it for western uses.

I spoke of the matter with a salesman of national prominence. He tells of using this secret, "I list fifteen names of possible prospects, that is persons who are interested in my product and are able to pay the price. Then I mentally make a sale to each person in the privacy of my room before I start out for personal calls."

"How does it work out?" I asked.

"About ninety percent in successful sales," he said. The salesman continued, "The secret seems to be this: you concentrate definitely on prospects, and then on individuals. You put in a few minutes each day picturing just what you want to take place, and then go out and hustle to accomplish that purpose. For example, if there is a difficult customer you desire to subdue, you create a mental-picture of yourself subduing him. You hold that picture steadily in your mind for ten minutes or so. A good time to focus your mind on major desires is while you are in the act of going to sleep, or while you are just waking in the morning. I find the best way to practice the procedure is to get off by myself, clear away from all noise and distractions, sit down and relax my mind completely, and then concentrate on the thing desired."

As a hypnotist, the thought crossed my mind as to how closely related this man's procedure was to the practice of autohypnosis. Maya may well be the power behind that phenomena. I wondered what some of the solemn Sages I had met would think of this westernizing of their methods. But "laws are laws," and operate whenever and wherever they may be applied.

If you have any special points you wish to present, it is well to present them in this mental rehearsal. Mentally visualize your client and talk to him mentally just as if he were actually physically present and the interview was real. Indeed, occultists claim that such an interview is "real" to a far greater extent than most people comprehend.

Having so prepared "the psychic path" in advance, proceed on to the actual interview, at which time this preparatory work will greatly increase the power of the silent psychic influencing at the in-person meeting.

Those experienced with the technique say it is best to think in terms of impulsion rather than compulsion over the other person. Compulsion is a force from without, while impulsion is a force from within. Compulsion might make an enemy of him; impulsion could make a friend of an enemy.

The method is simple. You do not try to compel the other person to do as you desire, rather you lodge the thought in his mind that he wishes to do as you desire. Or, one might say that the idea is to hold your thought on and for him, rather than to hold your thought over him. In this regard, when you wish to mentally influence the other person do not think in terms such as "You will do such and such." Rather concentrate your thought in the first person as if you were thinking for him, such as, "All right, I will do it at once." "Yes, I will make the purchase," etc.

And during the interview, as you talk to him, visualize your ideas strongly in your mind and well charged with prana (by thinking and willing it to be so), and then project the mental-image in the impulsion handling. Here in business, you are using precisely the same methods that you have learned for the performing of experiments in maya.

In the practical using of silent psychic influence, there is no need to stare into the eyes of the other man, nor to adopt a domineering manner. Instead, be calm, well poised, with an air of self-confidence, and speak with a tone of respect for the other man with a demeanor indicating politeness.

Your strength and power is of the inner realm, and remember the unspoken word is the most powerful—when you learn how to use it. "The Voice of the Silence" is the soundless sound prevailing over all loud sounding speech. It has been written by the Sages, *the silence is the workshop of the master magician; in it the great work is done; the rest is the mere materialization of that which already has been accomplished.*

The second phase of silent psychic influencing is in working with persons at a distance. This phenomena is no stranger to the West, as various kinds of "absent treatments" are well known. Practitioners of such often claim better results over a distance than when the treatment is given in person. Practitioners usually use the term "treat" in connection with an illness; I use the term in the more general sense of influence, in this text.

To "treat" a distant person psychologically, you simply project to him the previously visualized mental-picture of thought, well charged with prana, just as if he were actually seated or standing before you in person. The better you can sense the actual psychic presence of the other person, the more firmly established will be the psychic channel developed between you, and the greater the results of the psychic influence.

Psychic channel development may be achieved in several ways, in which you cause the distant person to be psychically present, i.e., producing a strong psychic awareness of the presence of the other person whose physical body is far removed in space. I might illustrate it by comparing such with the sight of a far away person seen through a powerful telescope; here the far distant person becomes "present" to your perception, to all intents and purposes. So, in the procedure of distant silent psychic influence, the distant person is brought psychically into your presence, and is placed in "psychic contact" with yourself.

In "distant treatments" you must use your visualizing faculties to such an extent that you can picture the other person as being before you—in person. The Hindu magicians use the crystal ball for this purpose. You can use it in the same manner to visualize him in the crystal. That is, you do not actually have to "see" him as you would a person in the physical body; you have merely to clearly "imagine" (image) him in this way. A modus operandi which will assist you in

141

establishing this psychic channel is to make use of what the Yogis call "The Astral Tube" in the process.

The Astral Tube is a device frequently employed by the real magicians of India. It consists of forming a tube-like "cleared path" psychically created in the akasa, enabling a free and ready passage of the projected thought-form and/or mental-picture to the mind of the other person. The Astral Tube is created by the thought and will along lines with which you are now familiar, viz., the thought creating the idea pattern of The Astral Tube by visualization, and the will forces it through space in the direction of the other person. Of course, the action of the will draws upon the prana, and presses it into service in the process.

The Astral Tube is psychically projected from the starting point of the crystal ball. You "see" and "will" its starting point there in the crystal, being sure to create a strong, positive, definite starting-point. Then, you must "see" and "will" the gradual projection, and elongation of the tube—something like a vaporous tube, or miniature tunnel, closely resembling the long extension tube of a telescope. This elongated tube is "seen" and "willed" as extending out until its end is lost in far-distant space. Then, when you experience that peculiar, subtle psychic "click" telling you that it has reached its destination, you must visualize the other person at the far end of the tube; then gradually draw back this picture to yourself until it seems to be in your actual presence. The Astral Tube is a secret of the East Indian magicians for concentrating and focusing their projections in silent psychic influence.

The successful establishment of "psychic channel rapport" with the distant person, either with or without The Astral Tube, results in a peculiar feeling of nearness to the other individual. As you practice, you will come to recognize the experience. Distance interposes no obstacles to the production of this rapport condition; it may be established half way around the world just as rapidly as with a person only a few miles distant.

Time and space are wiped out on the psychic plane, the magicians tell us.

After you begin experimenting, you will soon learn to recognize the peculiar "feeling" denoting that the psychic channel has been established. Practice repeatedly until you master this psychic skill of establishing this unique type of rapport, as it is essential to your influencing persons at a distance. Also, master the art of visualization in the crystal ball, as you have been instructed. With these two abilities under your control, you can effectively influence over vast distances; once the rapport is established, proceed exactly as if the individual you are working toward were with you in person. Finally, remember that in all cases of psychic influence, there must be an application of "The Threefold Yogi Formula," i.e., Visualization, Projection, and Affirmation! This formula is universal, and covers each and every case in all forms of psychic influence. It opens the doors of magic.

The Society of American Magician's "Ambassador of Magic," Benjamin J. Kleinman and his wife in front of the Royal Palace of the Maharaja of Mysore, India.

13
Yogi Mental Broadcasting

In addition to the manifestation of silent psychic influence in the direction of a particular person or persons, the Yoga teaching deals, also, with a broader application of the process in which a large field is covered, and sizeable groups of people are subjugated to the influence as a crowd. It is this handling that the magicians use in mass performances. I have named the phenomena, Yogi Mental Broadcasting, as being descriptive of the effects of this technique. As you will learn in studying the subject it has an even more personal aspect in relation to our daily lives and personal successes.

It is always easier to comprehend some comparatively unfamiliar phenomena when its operation is associated with a familiar one. For instance, persons just beginning to study thought transmission can grasp its principles best when these are associated with the idea of radio or television transmission. So, when I tell you that the Yogis state that psychic influence may not only be directed immediately to a certain person, just as a telegram may be sent to a particular individual, but that it may likewise be "broadcast" over a large area simultaneously; having these familiar associations before you, you will at once grasp the general nature of the processes manifested in mental broadcasting.

And there is another familiar feature which relates Yogi Psychic Broadcasting to radio or television broadcasting in that the former like the latter is picked up only by the proper instruments which are in tune to the correct waves lengths. In other words, psychic broadcasts are received only by the minds which are correctly tuned to receive them.

There is, however, an additional feature of this "psychic broadcasting" which has no corresponding feature in radio and television, and this is what the magicians know as "the law of mental attraction."

This "law" operates in the general direction of attracting to each other persons whose basic mental attitudes are attuned to the same psychic wave length. This tendency of humanity is well espressed in the old saying that "Birds of a feather flock together." This is definitely true, both in the physical world and in the psychic world as well.

This mutual attraction of the thoughts of different persons manifesting on the same general wave length operates in two basis ways, viz.: (1) it attracts to one the persons, things, circumstances, conditions, environment, events and happenings which are in vibrational harmony with your own thought, and (2) it attracts you to such persons, things, circumstances, conditions, events and happenings.

Whichever happens to be the line of the least resistance in the way of thoughts, feelings and desires will be the line of attraction manifested by "the law of mental attraction." Thus, according to this principle, either the other persons or things will be drawn toward you, or else you will be drawn towards them in response to this basic harmony. This is mental broadcasting.

Everyone, everywhere, is setting into operation, at all times, this law of mental attraction, but nearly always unconsciously, unstematically, and without definite purpose or direction. As an example, the man sending forth continuously gloomy and depressed thought vibrations will be found to attract to himself persons and things corresponding thereto. At the same time, he will be found to be drifting steadily towards persons and things corresponding to the general character of his thoughts and feelings, as sent forth in his constant mental broadcast.

In a like manner to the above example, the man sending forth thought vibrations of a hopeful and encouraging sort, will be found attracting to himself persons and things of a corresponding cheerful type, and will also be attracted to persons and thing so attunded to his general mental attitude.

You will observe that this principle works both ways: it attracts to us and us to them, not only the people and things which we earnestly desire, and for which we earnestly strive, but, also, the persons and things which we most fear and seek to avoid. All this occurring in direct ratio in the measure of our belief that they will come or happen to us. The strength of the blending of thought and belief determining the "attractice force" of that mental state. In this we have the specific operation of two seemingly opposing statements in the Scriptures which bear upon this subject, viz.: "As a man thinketh in his heart so is he." and "The things I have feared have come upon me." They are seen not to be opposing at all, but rather are the positive and negative operations of the same law.

Now, if the operation of "the law of mental attraction" can produce such powerful effects when it is used unconsciously, as it generally is, it is obvious that there are truly magical effects produced when purposely directed. Oriental wisdom provides that directive.

As Sadhu Parimal Bandhu instructed me in this matter while we were together in India. One should aim to "broadcast" clearly defined, specific messages, and thought currents instead of mental broadcasting indefinite thought-messages and waves and currents of mental attraction. The results can be amazing, and this teaching is one of India's most magical gifts to western people in telling of this knowledge.

The modus operandi of this productive mental broadcasting is to deliberately plan your thought-forms. Form the basis of Yogi Mental Broadcasting into clear mental-pictures showing exactly what you want, just when you want it, where you want it, and how you want it. They should constitute a mental demand—a psychic call for assistance!

145

America's master magician, The Great Virgil *photographing a troupe of Hindu snake charmers.*

Two Ambassadors of Magic (P. C. Sorcar, official magic ambassador of the government of India and Benjamin J. Kleinman, international ambassador for the Society of American Magicians) meet at Bangalore during "The all India Magic Congress."

Broadcast that call . . . and the call will be answered.

Remember, it is the rule of magic that nothing ever happens by chance; everything is under law and order! A part of that great universal law and order is that same law of mental attraction. When the magician deliberately puts that law into operation the results approach the miraculous. In fact, when you begin to put into operation Yogi Mental Broadcasting for yourself, the results will frequently be of such a surprising nature as to make one feel they are almost supernatural in origin. Of course they are not. All that occurs in the magic of

India is entirely the operation of the mystical laws of nature which you have put into activity through these practices.

It is important that you appreciate this point, nothing is ever supernatural, magic is but supernormal. Unless you plainly understand the natural character of these phenomena, you will fail to have that faith in Nature's powers which is necessary to enable you to draw upon her finer forces. "The Law of Attraction" operates here also. The drawing power of thought is made up of two elements, viz., the thought itself, and the element of faith in the efficacy of its power. The more you believe in and have faith in the natural laws of magic, the greater will the response be to that knowledge, and the more freely will these secret powers flow into you and be under your control. The real magicians of India have absolute faith in these powers.

In the performance of "mental broadcasting" you are really treating conditions, circumstances, and environment. Then you are projecting this mental-picture (thought form) into the Akasha, the ethereal substance of Nature. Here it will serve as an ideal pattern about which will materialize the conditions, circumstances, and environment you desire to have become realities. In addition, you are affirming the desirability of the changed condition, and your confident belief (faith) that the same will become materialized and actualized for you.

In this way, you create "a psychic magnet of idealized thought" which in turn sets into operation the "law of mental attraction" and the magical machinery thus set in operation will attract, draw, pull and push, in countless way, the things, persons, and conditions necessary to materialize the mental-picture which you have created and endowed with power.

Unexpected and unforseen things will begin to "happen." New things and persons will come into your life. New personal contacts will be made; new ideas will spring into your thoughts; new conditions and circumstances will form around and about you. Sometimes existing conditions may even be suddenly removed in order to make room for the newer and better ones which are being created for you by "the law of attraction."

In the performance of Yogi Mental Broadcasting you produce two different classes of results, viz., (1) you attract to yourself or you to them, or both, the persons who are fitted and adapted to cooperate with or serve you in the general manifestation of your ideals, plans, desires, and aims, as indicated by your mental ideal form set up by you in visualization, projection by your thought and will, and affirmed by your thoughts and words; and (2) you attract to you the things, that is the events, happenings, circumstances, and conditions which will fit into your general plans, aims, ambitions, desires, etc., or else yourself to these, or both. The Law of Attraction acts upon person and things alike.

You have already learned how persons may be reached by psychic influence, but you may wonder how inanimate "things" such as events, conditions, circumstances, etc. can be affected by thought and will. The question demands an answer, and the answer is forthcoming in the Yoga teachings, viz.:

It is held, you will recall, there are everywhere-present and everywhere-active the three universal principles of Akasha, Prana, and Creative Mind.

147

These three principles are held to be immanent and present in everything throughout the Universe. Also, it is held that there is no "mindless" thing in Nature. Everywhere, in everything, is there found mind and life, to some degree. The mind in the minerals, for example, serves to create the crystal-forms, which are as invariable and as regular as the forms of plant life and animal life; and that "indwelling mind" creates the ideal pattern around which the crystals form. The East Indian teaching further holds that in everything in Nature there is just enought mind to enable the created thing to manifest its nature, and do its work—no more, no less. Moreover, it is held that the lower degree of forms of embodied mind are negative to the higher ones, and may be moved, directed, and transformed by the will of an advanced mind.

There seems to exist a correlation between thoughts and things; a connection or rapport between them which causes things to move and act as the result of the direction of thought. Occultists insist that "thoughts are things and that things are thoughts of something." However one looks at it, it is accorded that things may be moved, transformed, and directed by thought.

This last is axiomatic and self-evident to all students of occultism, as, under the rule of the Hermetic Axion, "As above, so below; as within, so without; as in great, so in small," we are justified in believing that thoughts control and direct things. Consider some variety of applications:

The fabulous Humayun's Tomb of Delhi, India. This 16th century mausoleum designed of a striking blending of red and white sandstone and black and yellow marble, stands as a forerunner of the Taj Mahal. (Courtesy Government of India Tourism Office)

You may apply the process of Yogi Mental Broadcasting in a more general way in which a mental-ideal is visualized, projected, and affirmed as a "psychic call," as a mental demand for help and aid from all directions; or else you may employ the power in a more specialized manner, while still maintaining the character of "broadcasting." I will now indicate possible employment of this latter type which are of a personal nature.

Cases are on record in which merchants have greatly increased their business by the method of psychically "treating" the business for better conditions and circumstances. In such cases, the "treatment" has consisted simply of the clear visualization of the business in the desired condition, with crowds of people flocking in and buying merchandise, with shelves well stocked with salable goods, and with a good bank balance showing profit.

This visualization was positive. The projection was equally positive and hopeful. The affirmation was made with the firm conviction of its truth. Thus the ideal was thought of, seen, projected and affirmed as the initial stage of the materialization. And, in due corse, the ideal became real; the hope became fact; the dream became true!

And farmers have been known to visualize, project, and affirm the reality of good crops, ready markets, and satisfactory prices—and they achieved them! Also, persons seeking better positions have obtained them by the same process.

Again, professional persons, lawyers, physicians, artists, writers, and others transmute their ideals into realities by following the same general methods of the magicians of India. Men and women have found love and mates through the process of sending out a "psychic call" by means of mental broadcasting.

And so the story runs. I could report for your benefit case after case, incident after incident, personal experiences without end, all testifying to the efficacy of this form of psychic influence, Mental Broadcasting. But the important thing is that you try it for yourself.

The ancient teachings of India were not intended merely for past ages; they are as useful, valuable, and practical, now in the western world, as they were in the ancient oriental world. Natural laws do not change; they are eternal. As is written in venerable texts, "It is the same yesterday, today, tomorrow and forever." For the essential principles of Nature are over and above change, they cause changes but are not affected by change.

14

The Psychic Control
of Events

This chapter is basically an extension of the foregoing chapter. Here we will study in greater depth the mental controlling of circumstances and events.

As the Sages state, "That which you desire to become actualized on the physical plane must first be created in the mental plane." You have been instructed in how to exert this psychic influence over particular persons, and also how to "treat" general conditions and circumstances to psychically mold them as you wish them to be. I shall now give you the East Indian instructions of the magicians on how to influence events and happenings in order to have them occur—as you wish them to occur.

This type of performance is based upon the same rules of magic; the identical threefold Yogi method of visualization, projection and affirmation which you have learned so well. For, as I have told you, this method is universal to all magical handling of nature, and is designed to cover "all things desired" by the individual.

In the application of "the threefold method of mental magic" in the direction of controlling events, you really also apply it in the direction of influencing persons, conditions, and circumstances. You do this because events necessarily involve the actions of persons, and the creation of changes in conditions and circumstances. However, in specifically using the technique for this purpose, you concentrate upon "treating" the events, while bypassing special influencing of persons or conditions. Of course, as I mentioned, the control of events carries with it the control of certain persons and conditions, for the event is the happening; persons and conditions being simply the things to which changes happen in the event. As the magician instructs, "Control the happenings, and the rest are controlled by it."

An event is that which comes, arrives, or happens, due to the result of change. Every change is the result of causing forces, and every causing force implies the presence of some controlling power. Now, the dominant controlling power in psychic influence and mental magic is the creative power of your mind—and your mind is the instrument of you, yourself.

As you advance in your study of the real magic of India, you will learn more

150

of your Master-Self at the center of your selfhood. For the present, I ask that you rest assured that in your selfhood is a Master-Self—YOU—which is capable of employing your creative mind power in the direction of effecting those changes in things which constitute events, thus giving you the psychic control of events.

In all magical "treatments" to control events, you proceed along the general lines of (1) Visualization, (2) Projection, and (3) Affirmation, and in the process clearly, definitely, and positively "see" what you want to happen. You must positively and firmly project this mental-picture into the akasha (and simultaneously into the chitta of all persons concerned with the happening) with full faith and determination that it will happen exactly as you so visualize it. Finally, you must affirm, in the same determined spirit, that your mental-picture will become materialized and actualized in the physical world.

In the performance of Yogi Mental Broadcasting, as you have learned, your visualization becomes reality chiefly through the operation of the Law of Mental Attraction. In the manifestation of the psychic control of events, you set into operation the principle of Creative Will power. These two are not separate magic energies, but rather are the two opposite poles of the same basic psychic power. The one pulls, the other pushes; the one draws, and other drives. Each is powerful and of equal effect, but each has its own particular field of work to which it is especially adapted.

An ancient Hindu teaching regards the drawing power of the mind as "feminine;" the driving power of the mind being regarded as masculine. Occults say on the point, "The two poles of mind, i.e., desire and will, both are operative in the manifestation of occult power. Desire and will are active psychic forces, and both act and react upon the desire and will forces of others. The strong desire of the occultist is able to arouse the will of another mind, and may set up similar desire elements. The combined "will-desire" constitutes a powerful psychic battery, each pole of which is operative and effective, the combined power serving to attract and lure, and also to drive and compel, at the same time. This psychic power is the essence of all mental influence, and of all forms of the control by mind of persons or things, of conditions or events."

The Yogis carry this idea to even greater lengths, and on to higher planes of existence. They hold that the "Creative Mental Energy of the Universe" has two aspects—the male and the female, and symbolize this conception in the consorts or wives of the respective Deities. Hindu sages state of this as being the masculine principle of nature and the feminine principle of nature. The masculine principle is conceived as being akin to absolute will, while the feminine principle is conceived as being akin to infinite desire.

These two poles of psychic power are strongly active in the magical controlling of events.

In all psychic "treatments" intended to bring about desired events and happenings, it will be found that the crystal ball is the most effective instrument to employ as the focal center of concentration and visualization, and is used as a definite point of projection and affirmation. The positive and definite mental-picture may be developed and evolved much better in this way than through any other method. The Hindu magicians found this so centuries ago, and it still remains as truth.

151

Here is how to use the crystal ball for the psychic controlling of events:

First, "throw the mind blank," and after securing the right psychic condition, proceed to visualize the desired event, or that which you wish to happen. Make the mental-picture as clear and definite as possible; in connection with events, it will be well if you impart motion to it, and thus see the visualization in your "mind's eye" as a motion picture scene.

Having secured the proper moving mental-picture, project this into the akasha, and thus into the chitta, or "mind stuff" of all persons connected with the happening. This is done by projecting your mental-picture into space, and it will be reflected into the chitta of the various individuals who are destined to play parts in your psychic drama. Also, proceed to affirm positively the expected happening, employing words of authority.

The magicians state in connection with these instructions that it is well (prior to the commencing of the "treatment of events"), to charge one's being with prana via rhythmic breathing which will tend to give you an efficient control of the prana which you may then use to energize your projected thought-forms; you will finally reach the stage of development in which you can literally "feel" and "see" the projected thought-forms vibrating with the pranic energy which you have imparted to them. Also, if one has mastered Pranayama, and can arouse the Kundalini, or "serpent fire," it puts tremendous additional psychic power into the operation of "the threefold formula of the Yogi."

That you will readily be able to put these directions for the psychic controlling of events into operation, I will cite a case using such which will serve as an object lesson in the practice.

This case is of a well known editor and publisher of a magazine; now a very successful business woman whose work is known in many countries. She affirms that she owes her success to this technique.

She was of limited means, unknown to the public, and lacked training and experience in writing, editing, and publishing. But she had energy, and above all faith. Also she had acquired a knowledge of the principles and application of "the power of thought," which we have learned to call mental-magic.

She conceived the idea that she would like to edit and publish a magazine, and the more she thought about it, the more she wanted it. Finally, she reached the stage in which she felt that she just had to have a magazine of her very own publication. She didn't know how she was going to get it, but she felt if the principles of "thought power," she believed in, were true, they would work out this thing satisfactorily for her. If they couldn't or wouldn't then they were no good to her.

Like the poet, she said: "I care not just how fair she be, if she remains not fair to me." And she was right in this! Things are "good" only when they are good for something!

In that spirit, this woman started to work to materialize, objectify, and actualize that magazine. She began, naturally, with visualization, projection, and affirmation. She got so that she actually "saw" that magazine as a physical reality long before it became such. It seemed as real to her as her own home. In this strong conviction she had really created a most potent thought-form in the akasha, and had energized it with prana unconsciously. I say unconsciously

Sadhu Parimal Bandhu among devotees in India. (Photo reprinted with permission from RELIGIOUS MYSTERIES OF THE ORIENT pub. A. S. Barnes and Company, Inc 1975)

because her knowledge of the psychic process did not encompass the full knowledge of the matter that you have acquired in your studies.

And she dedicated herself to that magazine, day and night, unceasingly. She believed in it as she affirmed the fact of her own existence. In reality, she actually *thought and affirmed* that magazine into objective existence.

She had no money, she had no credit, she had no experience, she had no practical knowledge of editing or publishing. What she had was a vision. She had faith and an idea that was bound to become real. She had a hope that was determined to become a fact. She had a dream which was destined to become true. She had a burning desire for that magazine, and driving will-power to apply to its realization.

The "miracles" began to happen. Someone guaranteed her first printing bills. She got up the material for the magazine and sent out sample copies to names furnished her by friends. She got enough subscriptions to pay for the first issue, and to guarantee the payment for the second. This was but the beginning. From month to month, from year to year, she thought and affirmed that little magazine into a greater one; and then into a still greater; and so on and on. The magazine is now an international one with a vast reader coverage and magnificent advertising clientage. She has accumulated money, attained fame, and demonstrated success.

That is one woman's story who applied the principles of mental-magic and success became hers. Whatever your objectives, as the Sages express it, "Go ye and do likewise."

In passing, I might add that the very book you are reading (also *The Secret World of Witchcraft* and *Religious Mysteries of the Orient*) came into being in precisely the same manner. When Ron Ormond and I planned our journey into the Orient to search out the mysteries we had not the slightest idea as to how we

The Qutab Minar (The Tower of Love), Delhi, India. This graceful fluted tower of red sandstone, intricately carved and standing 234 feet in height, is known as "The Seventh Wonder of India." It was designed by the last Hindu emperor, Maharaha Prithvi Raj Chauhan, for his wife that she might climb to the top each day and see the Sacred River, Jumna. After a passing of eight centuries, visitors can still climb its steps safely. (Courtesy Government of India Tourist Office)

were going to accomplish our purpose. But we knew we had to make the journey to seek and find the hidden knowledge of eastern adepts and bring that knowledge back to our western culture. We dreamed about it, talked about it, thought about it day and night. Finally the journey into the unknown became a reality during which avenues were opened to us that had been closed for ages to occidentals. The knowledge became ours. It is true magic.

I could cite many outstanding examples of the successful use of this way of the magicians of India to psychically control events, but they would serve little further purpose. Rather let me suggest that you put these laws of magic into operation for yourself. You now have the "know how," so get to work and demonstrate the things for yourself. Say, "I can, I will, I dare, I do!" Then do it!, making yourself living proof of the ancient Yogi amphorism:

Make in your chitta the vritti-picture of that which you wish to come to pass. Repeat frequently the mantram of its coming to pass. Project into the akasha that picture, energized by prana, and crystalized by the mantram. Do these things, and that which you wish to come to pass will verily come to pass. Such is the law.

15
The Magic of Love

The student may well ask what has the subject of love to do in a book on magic? Remarkably, love-attraction is an important element in the repertoire of the magician. To the Yogis, love is perceived as a great cosmic law of attraction and activity, and they observe its action as influence and power throughout all Nature. Even the very word, "love" is oriental in origin, being derived from the ancient Sanskirt term, "lubh," meaning craving. The magicians hold that something akin to "male and female elements" may be found in everything, and state that there is an attraction between all different things, inorganic as well as organic, which is really in the nature of love.

Even spoken of is what may be considered as "the love of atoms." This is not as fanciful as it might seem at first, as the modern science of physics is now recognizing that all matter is composed of minute particles which possess opposite qualities which strongly suggest the respective ideas of "masculine" and "feminine." These terms are even employed in the laboratory.

The magicians hold that Creative Mind is the masculine element in magic while the Akasha is the feminine; the mating of these two producing magic. They claim that in love is found the possibility of the highest and profoundest manifestation. The Yogis state that love in its original essence is clean and pure, and that impurity comes only as a perversion by man. It is said that the misuse of any magical power is impure or "evil," while the proper use of the same natural principle is essentially "good." It is held that "all things are given man for his use, but nothing for his misuse." and "Everything is good for man to use, but nothing is good enough to use man."

The Yogis, also, beautifully illustrate and symbolize the humble origin of love, and the glorious heights which it attains in its nobler forms, in their adage: "Love is like the lotus; it has its roots in the dark soil of the riverbed; its stalk and stem rest in the muddy waters of the stream; its leaves lie upon the bosom of the waters; but its flower lives in the clear, pure air, and faces the sun."

Without love, all of Nature's creative work would perish and would never be renewed. It is not only true that " 'Tis love that makes the world go 'round;" it is equally true that " 'Tis love that makes and remakes the world, and keeps it going." Scholars have had much to say about the universal living force, the "Will to Live;" but they might well have called it the "Will to Love," for without "loving" there would be no "living." The chief activity and manifestation of this Will to Live consists in sex-attraction and manifestation, through all of nature, high and low. Equal in force with self-preservation, as a basic law in nature, is the law of love, for living creatures commonly risk life in pursuit of their mates.

Emerson says, "The lover seeks in marriage his own private felicity and perfection, and no prospective end. But nature hides in his happiness her own end—the perpetiuity of the race. We are made alive and kept alive by the same means."

To understand the power of the love instinct in men and women, we must go back to the beginnings of the human race. Deep in the nature of every man and every woman, there are powerful forces of emotional order, great instinctive latent desires awaiting their time to manifest themselves. When they stir into activity, in response to the proper stimulus, they cause the eyes to brighten and the heart to throb. Their subtle aroma mounts to the brain of the man and woman, and they see strange sights, hear strange sounds, and dream strange dreams.

In the fact of Nature's "will to live," which is really her "will to love," is found the explanation of the tremendous force of love attraction. Here is to be found the great secret of life. Nature is back of the love instinct in every way; she wants the lovers to win.

Psychic love-influence is one of the most potent forms of psychic influence because Nature is backing the influence. In the "libido," as it is called by psychologists, is found the great unconscious realms of emotional energy in which abide the potent love-impulses. Our unconscious thoughts are infinitely more far-reaching than are those of our conscious mind in affecting our spontaneous behavior, as conscious mental process, (such as directed by thinking), are of comparatively recent origin in evolution. On the other hand, the unconscious processes which are manifested in instinctive action have a heritage since the very dawn of man.

Now in relation to the performance of magic, the effects of psychic influence is largely produced upon the unconscious or subconscious planes of the mind. When the psychic seed thus implanted in subconscious mental fields reach the blossoming stage, then their activities reach the conscious field of the mind. Many such subconscious seeds ready for sprouting lie planted in the mind. Supply the right conditions and they blossom quickly into the realm of consciousness, and proceed to bear fruit. The field of the mind of persons of both sexes is filled with material for an abundant growth in the "garden of love." And the conditions for producing this growth may be supplied from the physical plane, such as due to personal contacts, or they may arise from projected influence on the psychical (astral) plane, which is the realm of the magician.

Like the inductive power of electricity, which is able to arouse by "induction" a similar state from one magnetic field to another, so the love vibration (via psychic influence) is capable of arousing by induction a similar rate of vibrations in the emotional nature and subconsciousness of another person of the opposite sex coming within the "field of emotional induction."

This "field of emotional induction" is called by the magician, love-energy. It is like a storage battery—a stored-up reservoir of love. Love-energy is like a bolt of lightning seeking instinctively for a point to "strike" and discharge its energy.

Bharat Natyam is an exquisite temple dance of Southern India. In times of antiquity, dancers were attached to temples, but today it is no longer a part of temple ritual. In this picture, the dancer is poised in the Natraj pose. Natraj is revered as the king of dancers whose bronze statue in the foreground presents him dancing "the cosmic dance of the universe."

Now this objective upon which the love-energy may "strike" does not necessarily have to be a person of the opposite sex; it can be events, circumstances, conditions, etc. as well. The magicians most frequently employ it this way, providing, as it does, a tremendous battery of psychic power in nature. I will tell you methods for this application shortly, but, first, I will cover further phases of Love-Attraction for your understanding.

The love-energy is capable of "hypnotizing" the individual, in a sense. We commonly hear this expressed as "love is blind"—the object loved by the lover being seen through a mist of fantasy in highly idealized form. Also, it is very possible to be in love with love, which produces the same psychic blindness to reality. These also are factors made use of by the magician in the performance of magic.

In the ancient Atharva Veda is found a statement concerning this love with love factor. Translated, it is written:

"O my children, be not self-deceived. What you think is the long-waited-for loved one is merely a puppet which you have dressed up in the fanciful garments of your ideal loved one. As the coiled-up rope, seen in the twilight, is mistaken for the serpent; as the trail of journeying ants is mistaken for the crack in the earth; so is this stranger mistaken for him or her whose picture abides in your heart. You see such a one, not as he or she really is, but as you have dreamed of your ideal loved one as being. You are not in love with this one or that one; you are in love with your ideal one. The one before you is as but a thought-form projected by you upon the Akasha, or a reflection of Maya."

In addition to the presence of these subtle but powerful special elements in the manifestation of love-attraction, there are also present other special elements of semi-physical character in nature which must be taken into consideration in the study of this subject. I allude to that peculiar form of attractive force in which the psychical and the physical seem to meet and blend—that attractive force which is known as Sexual Magnetism.

That there is present an active attractive force between individuals of opposite sexes, which seems to proceed along the lines of the universal Law of Polarity, there can be no doubt. The males and females of the same species are attracted toward each other in the psycho-physical way similar to that manifested in the attraction between positive and negatively charged particles of magnetized matter.

The Yogis have long recognized this subtle force of sex-magnetism. They claim that it is a form of prana colored with strong emotional vibrations; or, if you prefer, it is strong emotional currents charged with prana; in either case, it is a combination of emotion and prana. The Yogis pay great attention to this sex-magnetism, not only in relation to its basic purpose, but to tramsmute it into Ojas, or high form of mental/physical energy, to be used for other purposes such as brain stimulation, etc.

It is this transmuted sex-magnetism combined with the love-energy that is used in connection with magic, as an additic al source of power.

Speaking of sex-magnetism, Swami Viveknanda says, "The Yogis affirm that part of the human energy which is expressed as sex-energy easily becomes

The magic of the dance in India. Dancing is an art from in India that echoes the temple sculptures. The above photo shows a lovely Kathak dancer in a characteristic pose. Kathak is a form of north Indian dancing made popular in the Muslim courts. Kathak dancers can duplicate with the aid of anklets with bells (as shown here) the most intricate rhythms on the drum. The photo below presents a pose from the Rani Karna, an Orissi dance from Eastern India.

changed into Ojas; the Yogi pays particular attention to that center, and tries to take up this sexual energy and convert it into Ojas, and Ojas is as food for the Kundalini, the Serpent Power."

It will be seen in love-attraction there is held to be two active and powerful elements, viz.: (1) the element of Sex Magnetism, in which there is radiated from one individual to another of the opposite sex a subtle magnetic-type energy akin to physical magnetism, and tending to set up by induction in the other person a similar rate and character of vibration. Further, this sex-magnetism may be transmuted into Ojas, which as food for the Kundalini intensifies the psychic powers. (2) the element of love-energy can be directly manifested in psychic influence, and provides the magician with additional power in his control over the finer forces in Nature.

Continuing, the element of sex-magnetism in love-attraction is found to be a special form of the Kundalini principle. The Yogis hold that the subtle energy of "The Serpert Power" is closely connected with the creative energies, the sex energies of the body. This being the case, it follows that rhythmic breathing, (according to the Yoga Methods), accompanied by concentration upon the Muladhara Chakra, or Psychic Lotus, located at the base of the spine, at the lower end of the Sushumna Channel, will tend to arouse and render active the Kundalini there abiding in a dormant state.

In connection with such rhythmic breathing and concentration upon the Kundalini Center in the Muladhara, the Yogis alternate sittings for the purpose of concentrating upon the higher aspects of love. In this practice, the Yogis employ the crystal ball as a focal center of concentration, and "hold the thought" of love in its higher phases, i.e., in its affectional phases, rather than in its purely physical phases.

Following the symbolism of the Hindu allegory, you should "hold the thought" of the Lotus Flower of Love rising in the clean, pure air, and facing the sun   rather than of the dark material soil of the riverbed in which the roots of the Lotus are embedded. The Yogis find no need to stir up this rootsoil, nor the roots themselves as they are innately powerful. Instead, concentrate, as do the Yogis, upon the higher expression of the beautiful Lotus Flower of Love, for that is the part of your love-nature which requires the greatest development. As such the master magicians search, for to acquire the highest power the love within must possess an inner fineness. Think of this as a burning Sun of Love within your soul, which though unseen by the physical eye is yet powerfully present to the "inner eye" of others. The pure blending of the elements of psychic influence and sex-magnetism in oriental love-attraction brings greatness to the magician.

The manifesting and expressing of The Magic of Love, as used by the magician, is a special form of application of the combined principles of visualization, projection, and affirmation which is universal to "magic formula." By combining this with the power of Sex Magnetism, a most powerful form of psychic influence or mental-magic is produced. According to Yoga teachings, the love-energy adds power to magic, and the "love objective" provides an astral "lightning rod" which attracts unerringly the psychic projection of the magician. Such is the Magic of Love.

161

The Great Taj Mahal (The Temple of Love), Agra, India. This renowned shrine was built in 1629 by the Hindu emperor, Shah Jahan, in memory of his favorite wife, Mumtaz Mahal. This huge structure of white marble resting on red sandstone is literally a jewel, and took 22,000 Artisans and craftsmen seventeen years to construct. Marble was brought from one part of India, red sandstone from another, and semi-precious stones from all over Asia. Inlay work with jasper, agate, lapis lazuli, carnelian and bloodstone was done so skillfully that neither the sense of touch nor even a magnifying glass can detect breaks between two stones. It was designed to surpass anything the world had ever seen before or ever would see again in monumental beauty.

Sarcophagus inside the Taj Mahal. Incredible as it seems, the finely filigreed screen, looking like lacework, is marble. The other ornamentations are inlays of different kinds of marble and precious stones in white marble. Moslem art depends, to a great extent, on exquisite abstract ornamentation, since Moslem religous law forbids the representation of gods or human figures.

The Love Magic has its place between men and women, and also in relation to things which likewise carry these elements of polarity. Use the crystal ball as your focus of concentration for whatever your purpose may be, and along with your projection, direct also, the love-energy and sex-magnetism towards that which you desire, wish, crave, long for, and seek to have manifested in actuality in your own life, and induce in others.

Concentrate upon the ideals which you wish to become real; the hopes which you wish to become fact; the dreams which you wish to become true. Use your combined psychic influence of love attraction as follows: (1) to make yourself be or do what you wish to be or do; (2) to make happenings and events occur as you desire them to occur; (3) to make conditions and circumstances what you wish them to be; (4) to make your environment and surroundings as you want them; (5) to bring love into your life.

Also do unto others, in like manner, as you would have done unto yourself.

The Magic of Love produces a very personal kind of psychic influence. Perform always as A White Magician, keep your character noble, your goals lofty, and your purposes high. Make these principles of magic your "way of life," and greatness will be yours as a Master Magician.

16

The Secrets of Yoga Cosmology

Yoga Cosmology is Astral Plane Magic. It is listed among the High Magics, and includes the extra sensory perception powers which are considered of vast importance to the magician. In the book, *Religious Mysteries of the Orient*, Ron Ormond and I touched on the subject of Hindu clairvoyance as Parimal Bandhu explained it to us. In this chapter and the next, I will cover this subject in depth in relation to our study of the real magic and mysticism of India.

Certain phases of Cosmology have direct relationship to an understanding of occult and magical phenomena in the Universe. It affirms the Yoga teaching that infinite space is filled with a subtle, ethereal substance known as Akasha which is more tenuous than the most tenuous matter we can possibly conceive, and can only be described by the terminology of "infinitely thin, rare, and light," as an ancient Hindu text informs us.

I have brought you acquaintanceship with this etheral substance before, which I. will now cover in more detail in connection with Yoga Cosmology.

It is held that in the infinite substance of the akasha there exist what are called "The Akashic Records." These are records of past happenings and events which are imprinted on the ethereal substance of the akasha just as truly as the events of the present may be photographed on motion picture film. Indeed, the magicians say, these records may be reproduced for viewing in a manner closely resembling the showing of a motion picture.

As Sadhu Parimal Bandhu explained it, "Everything that has ever happened, every event, every occurrence, every action, is represented by a series of records on the substance of the Universal Akasha which pervades all space. On the planes of the Akashic Records there exist imperishable records of every happening that has ever occurred in the Universe. The Askashic Records represent the 'memory' of the universal substance, just as the records in the brain cells of a person can store away memories, or a computer can have its memory banks.

"As I have acclaimed, in the great memory banks of the Universe are registered and stored away these infinity of records of all that has gone before in history. He who by proper development of his powers is able to gain access to these records can read them like the pages of a book. Just as the modern motion picture film records and reproduces pictures of events which may be reshown in times when the original events are long since gone, so The Akashic Records register pictures, open to those who can gain access to them, which reproduce the sights of the things and actions which have long since passed away from the material scene."

The Yoga teaching on the matter of The Akashic Records is that the Infinite Akasha, filling all space, is permeated with the Infinite Universal Mind/Principle; where one is, the other must be for they are twin aspects of infinite reality. Consequently, there is an infinite memory in this Universal Mind/Principle, which is embodied in the Universal Akasha/Principle. Thus, according to Yoga teaching, the Cosmos is really seen as an "infinite brain," having its material substance and base, and its indwelling and immanent psychic or mental principle.

To express this principle in a direct manner, one might say that every event

The Great American Illusionist, Lee Grabel performing the classical "levitation illusion." This effect, which is based upon the real magic of India, has become a feature in the shows of leading magicians of the world.

or happening, every scene and action is perceived by the Universal Mind of the Cosmos, and is registered eternally in the universal ethereal substance, called the Akasha, where it forever abides in the condition of a "memory."

There is however an observation to be made here in regard to this explanation. The words "forever" and "eternal" are not here employed in the occidental sense of the terms, i.e., being of beginningless and endlessness. The Yoga teaching is that there has been and will be an infinite number of "eternities," each extending over countless years, then passing away. Then, after countless years of nonactivity, being succeeded by a new "eternity" in which new chains of worlds will come and go. At the end of each of these "eternities," the teaching state, The Akashic Records of the past "eternity" are wiped off the cosmic blackboard, as it were, and the cosmic memory fades away in the dreamless sleep of the Universal Mind/Principle, to be succeeded by a new cosmic memory upon the subsequent awakening. Each eternity being known as a Maja-Kalpa.

The oriental teaching, therefore, holds that in the cosmic memory of The Akashic Records are to be found the full, complete, clear and perfect records of the present Maja-Kalpa. These records are preserved in perfect condition, and may be perceived and read by the magicians who have trained their extra sensory perceptive powers. Some of these Akashic Records may be sensed readily, even by the psychic powers of an initiate, while others are extremely difficult and must be probed by an Adept; between these two extremes are countless phases and degrees of records and the ability to ready them.

The student may ask the question as to just where are these Akashic Records stored; just where are they to be sought? To answer that question, one must understand the oriental teaching about "planes of existence," as they are called. One must not jump to the conclusion that a "plane" is a place, as in Yoga instruction, a "plane" is a "rate, state, or condition of vibration" and not a "place" at all. Every point in space has many planes of existence manifesting upon it. To understand this, think in terms of light waves, heat waves, sound waves, radio waves, etc. which abide in the same point of space, without intefering with each other.

Now, the Yoga instruction continue that The Akashic Records abide and are stored upon that particular "plane" of cosmic activity which is known as The Astral Plane. The Astral Plane abides in all space; in fact it is one of the several particular planes in infinite space. So The Akashic Records are seen to be wherever there is akasha, and akasha is everywhere! The storehouse of The Akashic Records, therefore, is infinite. The seeker for these records accordingly does not have to travel to some particular place to read them; instead of seeking a "place," the record-seeker must take the necessary steps to penetrate The Astral Plane. Once his psychic vision functions on that plane, the rest is merely a matter of detail for him.

Once on The Astral Plane, the initiate may still ask, to which place on that plane do I go to read the records ? One goes to no "place" because on The Astral Plane finite space and time are wiped out, inasmuch as thought travels from one point of space to another immediately on The Astral Plane, thus one is practically present in all space at the same moment. Thought, like gravitation on the physical plane, is omnipresent on The Astral Plane. Once the magician pierces the veil of The Astral Plane, he is, to all practical intents and purposes, present at every point on that plane at the same time. He may travel from one point of space to another in an instant; he may proceed from one point of time to another immediately.

The clairvoyant magician, on The Astral Plane, coming in contact with The Akashic Records, and learning how to "read" them, performs an apparently simple, but really quite a complicated psychic action. The Akashic Records of a particular scene or happening closely resemble the continuous film of a motion picture; you will recall the simile. Instead of the countless films being attached to each other in the form of a continuous length, the "films" of The Akashic Records are superimposed one over the other, like layers or strata. The thought of the clairvoyant travels instantaneously through these superimposed layers, and thus *sees* the whole scene reproduced like the picture on the screen, or rather, as it originally occurred in actual happening in past time, as the case may be.

The 20th Century electronic engineer will note how close this psychic process of scanning the layers of The Akashic Records is to a modern computer which scans its "memory discs" to locate its stored material.

The highly developed and thoroughly trained magician (clairvoyant) "sees" the process of an ancient event just as he would see the action of a play on the stage, or a motion picture on the screen. He is able to shift the scene at once, at will; for on The Astral Plane to think of anything is to bring it instantly before yourself. The magician though, has no power to alter the action of the event, for that is a true reproduction of an actual occurrence that once took place on the stage of the physical (material) plane. All that he can do in the way of control or change is to control the rate of speed at which the pictures of the drama pass before his gaze. He can make the "astral film" of The Akashic Records run fast or slow, or even make it hold immovable on any one scene for any desired length of time, in a manner remarkably similar to modern television camera technique.

The astral plane magic of reading The Akashic Records is truly wonderful magic, and the records furnish an endless source of knowledge for the adept clairvoyant. The great dramas of the past are spread before the magician. By a mere effort of thought and will, he is able to focus his psychic gaze upon any particular picture of the world's history that he may select.

As clairvoyance is an astral plane phenomenon, all forms of clairvoyance can pursue The Akashic Records; each seer developing his favorite method. In the next chapter, I will instruct you in the Hindu technique of clairvoyance. We will now study further of the phenomena that lies within Yoga Cosmology, the Magic of the Astral Plane.

The class of clairvoyant phenomena which deals with the probing of events destined to come to pass in future time is unique. There can be no Askashic Records of future events, for these have not as yet happened, and so cannot have been recorded. The Yoga teaching on this matter is based upon the two following facts, viz., (1) the existence of a Universal Mind/Principle, and (2) the existence of the Law of Cause and Effect. The Hindu Sages hold that in the Universal Mind there is present the power to see clearly the particular effects

Various forms of popular magic in India. Upper photo shows magic on the streets of Calcutta during the famous Shiva Festival, while lower photograph shows magic inside on the stage of the Empire Theater during a presentation of the Hindu illusion "Stretching a Girl."

due to following existing causes, and, in this way, to see the future effect as part of the present cause. In other words, it may be said of the perception of future events that to the Universal Mind/Principle there is the perception of "coming events casting their shadows before" combined with the power to see clearly the nature of existing causes and the character of the effect which are certain to arise therefrom. Probed by clairvoyance these can be perceived.

As an illustration, consider the situation where a man is gazing through a microscope and sees "coming" certain happenings which would be entirely beyond the observation of the microscopic creatures to which the "happenings" are bound to occur. If a man had the ability to know and perceive with certainty the presence of all the existing causes in the world, it would be possible for him to predict the effects which were bound to follow in due time. Following this conclusion through, we have an understanding of the operation of future-time clairvoyance.

On The Astral Plane of the akasha, also, are found the astral colors, the auras, the thought-forms, and similar semi-physical manifestation of thought. To the clairvoyant vision of the magician who is properly developed, these astral phenomena are as plainly discernible as are the physical phenomena perceived on the physical plane. All such phenomena are entirely the results of the manifiestation of higher rates of vibration of Nature's Finer Forces, and are absolutely natural in character.

There remains one other important phase of Yoga Cosmology to be discussed, which is present-time-distant psychic perception. Here the element of time is not involved, as in the case of other forms of clairvoyance which have been described. The action is in the present time, but the element of space is involved. In this form of clairvoyance, the magician is able to sense events occurring at some distant point in space. Here the ordinary limitation of space are wiped out by the ESP powers.

How?

The Yoga teaching are quite explicit concerning this, and affirm that every material thing has it astral counterpart. This is true of everything from the tiniest particle of material substance on to any place, scene, or changes underwày in the physical world. The clairvoyant's psychic perceptive powers, proceeding on The Astral Plane, does not see the actual physical things and the movements thereof, but rather the astral counterpart of such things and movements. It is as though The Astral Plane were a gigantic mirror in which is reflected everything that occurs in the physical world in the most minute detail. This being so, it is seen that any mind capable of functioning on the astral plane is able to discern this "reflected" astral image of each and everything occurring on the physical plane.

As you have been instructed, remember, space is wiped out on The Astral Plane. To clairvoyant thought it is but necessary to "think" of a distant place in order to "be there" on the astral plane, and to perceive the "associated astral images" of that place and scene immediately, as though the observer were actually present in physical form at that location. Thus, while the body of the magician remains in its original position on the physical plane, his thought on the astral plane is able to project itself to any desired point in space; and, once there, he is able to see astrally, by means of the astral senses (which I shall describe in the next chapter), all the events occurring at that place or scene.

In some forms and phases of clairvoyance there appear to be manifested the ability of magnifying or diminishing the size of the pictures of the things perceived. Skilled psychic claim to be able to perceive minute forms such as one would see through a microscope. Likewise, they have been able to reduce the size of vision of far-off scenes so that a very large area is included in the picture.

When you grasp the basic principles of astral perception which lie within the Cosmology of Yoga, you will be able to appreciate the "Seven Powers of the Yogis" which are stated in the ancient Hindu teaching, as follows:

"The Yogi acquires seven astral powers resulting from the proper application of Samyamam (1) the power of psychically seeing into the form of minute matter; (2) the power of unlimited reach; (3) the power of knowing of the past; (4) the power of perceiving what is yet to occur; (5) the power of great will; (6) the power of influencing physical things; (7) the power of astrally going anywhere at will.

Such are the powers related to Astral Plane phenomena which are of the High Magic. They are powers of the Master Magicians.

17
Becoming A Master Magician

In this supplemental chapter to the foregoing, I will tell you of The High Magic Of India (of which all other forms of magic are but imitations), and how to develop the powers of Yoga Cosmology. This is the type of magic which is performed in secret monastaries in the mountains of Northern India and Tibet by the Adepts. This magic is in no sense supernatural, but it is decidedly supernormal, and shows a most amazing control over the forces of Nature. I will both describe the effects of such high magic and give you the modus operandi so you will know of the means of developing as do the Master Magicians.

As you have studied, there are three kinds of magic seen in India. One is the fakir type which the tourist enjoys. However it is but a presentation of clever trickery. Then there is the magic of the intermediate magician in which is employed the particular form of oriental hypnotism known as Maya; the spectators thinking they see what is in fact unreality. Third, there is the supernormal magic of the Adepts, which, while apparently defying the laws of nature and seeming to accomplish the impossible is nonetheless actually occurring before the eyes of the beholders. This is the High Magic.

You will note that I use the words "apparently defying the laws of nature and seeming to accomplish the impossible" because nothing ever really defies Nature. The Adept produces his magic by controlling nature in advanced ways unsuspected by the average person. To accomplish this magical purpose, the Adept employs exactly the same principles of magic which you have learned, but to such a degree has he advanced his powers that his visualization projected upon the akasha, held firm by unshakable will, and energized by highly concentrated prana is sufficient to cause an actual materialization in the substance of the akaska, bringing forth a unique physical occurrence which to the uninitiated seems most magical in nature. This is the modus operandi of the

High Magic. This type of magic has never been scientifically studied, but more than 50,000,000 human beings in the Orient testify to it.

As I have commented, these Adepts hold that there is absolutely nothing supernatural about the powers employed or the effects produced. They assert positively that the power and the effect are purely "advanced nature," and come fully under natural law and order. The fact is that there are certain Finer Forces of Nature, unknown to the masses of people, but known to certain advanced minds of the race. These forces are employed to perform these apparent "miracles" known to the Yogis and their students, and to those who have been permitted a glimpse "behind the veil." You have had that glimpse.

As an instance of how an effect of High Magic has been imitated, recall the "Mango Tree Trick" of the fakir, and the deceptive way it was accomplished. In an Adept's performance of this same effect, there occurs a real and actual rapid growth of the planted seed. How is this possible without violating natural laws? The explanation is in the skilled employment of prana, projected and held firm by the concentrated thought and will of the magician; nature being compelled to "speed up" her processes in the development of the tree from the seed, and fruit from the tree. None of her process are changed, but have merely been speeded. Using a familiar illustration, it might be said that Nature's film of the whole process, in such cases, was run at a highly increased rate of speed, and the picture on her screen was rushed through in a few minutes, instead of the many days required for the performance when the film was run at the regulation speed. That is the secret.

Another effect performed by the Adepts is to make fish-eggs hatch in a few minutes. Again the secret lies in speeding up the normal processes of nature. Unless the mango seed had been alife and perfect, no magical power could have grown a tree from it. Unless the fish-eggs had been properly fertilized and alive, there could have been no fish hatched from them by any magician. The whole natural process of growth was performed by the vital forces of plant and egg, just as in the normal growth   the only difference being the "speeding up" of the process, or running faster the vital film. Nature gives us many familiar illustrations of the fact that time is relative, not absolute, in natural processes. Some seeds sprout faster than do others; some eggs hatch more rapidly. A tiny insect is born, matures, breeds, lays eggs, and dies, all in the space of a single day.

Another mystery of the High Magic is for the Adept to hold a container of cold water between the palms of his hands, and by employing the power of projected prana to cause it to boil. In this experiment, the magician concentrates intently upon the water. Soon there is noted a peculiar ebulition, bubbling, and "boiling" in the water; tiny bubbles forming at the bottom and sides of the recepticle and then mounting to the top. In every way, there is the appearance of the application of great heat, yet the water actually remains cold to the touch. You will recall how this effect has been imitated by the fakirs by using a tricky brass bowl with double sides.

A demonstration of High Magic of a somewhat similar nature is performed by certain Adepts in which the magician produces what seems to be a process of "refrigeration by evaporation," lowering the temperature of a jar of water by a

The above photo shows a Hindu magician performing a stage version of the Levitation mystery.

marked number of degrees. In this case, the open jar of water, composed of clay and quite common in tropical countries, is wrapped with cloths saturated with water, and is held in the hands of the magician, whose attention is then closely concentrated upon it. The prana is thus projected into the moistened cloths surrounding the jar, and evaporation is produced in the water moistening the clothes. Such evaporation produces a certain fall in the temperature of the jar, and the interior water becomes cooler.

That the procedure follows purely natural laws is evidenced by the fact that in many tropical countries water is habitually cooled by placing it in an earthen jar surrounded with moistened cloths, and placing it in the sunlight; evaporation and consequent refrigeration thus resulting. Here, however, the prana of the magician takes the place of the sun's rays, and in some strange manner produces an evaporation of the water saturating the clothes, and thus lowers the temperature of the interior water. The feat is wonderful magic, but it will be seen to proceed in exact accordance to Nature's well established laws, and not contrary to them.

The ability to control the temperature of their body is a feat often performed by the Adepts. In Tibet, cases are reported of the exponents of High Magic sitting for long periods of meditation in the freezing cold in perfect comfort; the snow actually melting about their body.

173

Another amazing effect of the High Magic is that of levitation, or the act of raising one's body, or the body of another, up into the air where it remains unsupported.

In the performance of this feat of levitation, the body, under the control of the magician, is seen to rise slowly in the air apparently defying gravity. The Adepts assert that the phenomenon is genuine, and is caused by a particular application of prana, directed and controlled by rhythmic breathing, which in some unknown way counteracts the pull of gravity and raises the body against such pull.

The principle of rhythmic breathing is held to play an important part in the production of the phenomenon of levitation. One is here reminded of the familiar feat of our western lands, in which the body of a heavy person is lifted easily from the ground upon the fingertips of several persons who are breathing in rhythmic union. Possibly the "key" to levitation might be found by following up this significant lead.

The Hindu magicians, themselves, say that they do not understand "just why" the body is raised into the air during the act of rhythmic breathing in this special way, but they do know how to apply the method. Parimal Bandu mentioned that only certain magicians seem able to achieve the "knack" of levitation, the remainder never being able to accomplish it, no matter how carefully they are instructed.

From what information I could glean about levitation, the phenomenon is produced by creating a strong mental picture of one's body (or the body of another) rising in the air, then projecting a strong current of prana in such a way as to neutralize the pull of gravitation, and, at the same time, performing a certain form of rhythmic breath, which is said to be the real secret of the process. They claim that they are greatly fatigued after a feat of this kind, which would seem to indicate that the will is actively employed in the technique.

I sought for more knowledge about levitation, but that is all I was able to learn of the process. So striking is the effect of levitation that it has become a much imitated feat. Indeed, occidental stage magicians have designed conjuring methods of producing the effect, and "The Floating Lady" has become a featured illusion in many shows. The celebrated magician, Howard Thurston, on returning from his tour in India, developed the illusion and made a sensation of it in his performances. Many other magicians have since done likewise. The famous American illusionist, Lee Grabel even advanced the idea of levitation in his show to the extent of causing a girl playing a piano to float up from the stage; girl and piano then turning a complete somersault in midair. Levitation remains as one of the great mysteries of magical illusions.

We will now consider Yogi Astral Plane Phenomena, which belongs to the High Magic; these powers continue our study of Yoga Cosmology and take us into the realm of extra sensory perception.

Simplest of the Yogi's psychic abilities is that known as telepathy. This phenomenon consists of the conscious projection and reception of the vibratory thought waves emanating from the minds of persons performing the processes of thought. The Yogis hold that there is always more or less unconscious telepathy in operation among people. Everyone is constantly emanating thought waves,

174

and everyone is constantly receiving such; but the performance is chiefly along unconscious lines. The conscious projection and the conscious reception of these thought vibrations constitutes the psychic phenomena of telepathy. The Yogis hold mastery of the skill as elemental.

Higher in the scale of the Yogi's supernormal powers is that class of psychic phenomena known generally as clairvoyance, or psychic perception. In this class of phenomena, the mind functions on the astral plane, rather than upon the ordinary physical plane. That is to say, the mind employs its "astral senses" rather than its "physical senses," and its objects so perceived by these astral senses are the associated astral images rather than the ordinary physical objects of which these astral images are the counterparts or reflections. You have been informed concerning these "astral images" in the preceding chapter, so you will have this understanding.

The "astral images" cannot be perceived by means of the five physical senses, but may only be sensed by employing the "astral senses." The "astral senses" are the counterparts of the five physical senses in everyway excepting that while the physical senses function on the physical plane, the astral senses function on the astral plane. The description and use of these astral senses constitutes an important phase of the Yoga teaching.

Swami Ramavedananda says, "Man has, in addition to the five physical senses, the corresponding counterparts of these, known as the five astral senses. By means of these astral senses he is able to see, hear, feel, taste, and smell on the astral plane in response to the stimuli of the astral counterparts of his physical organs, though which the astral sensations reach the consciousness. The astral senses are inactive and dormant in the majority of human beings, but may be rended active and operative by means of the approved methods of psychical development, chiefly through the practice of Pranayama."

Before proceeding to a more detailed consideration of the activities of these astral senses, I would call your attention to the fact that in the majority of cases there are only two of the five astral senses employed in psychic perception or clairvoyance, i.e., the astral sense of sight, and that of hearing. In fact, the astral sense of sight is frequently the only one manifesting effects, that of hearing being far less common. The use of the astral sense of hearing is known as clairaudience, literally "clear hearing." There are no distinctive terms applied to the three other astral senses, for, as I have said, their use is infrequent.

In clairvoyance, the person penetrates the veil of the astral plane, and there perceives the "astral images" of physical objects in actual existence on the physical plane; or else he perceives the pictures of past events in the Akashic Records; or else he perceives representations of "the Universal Mind" which indicate future happenings necessarily resulting from present condition and causes. In clairvoyance, also, by means of the astral senses, the person perceives the Auras (the astral colors), and the various thought-forms which are produced in the Astral World by the action of the thought of individuals on the physical plane.

Clairvoyance is developed by the Yogis in various ways and by different methods. The Hindus are inclined to favor the course of gradual development

Premier illusionist, Lee Grabel, presenting his sensational version of levitation, "The Floating Piano." (Courtesy The Grabel Mystery Extravaganza)

and unfoldment by means of the use of the crystal ball in concentration. They also favor accompanying this practice by the methods of Pranayama, including, of course, the exercise of rhythmic breathing.

The Yogis teach that in relation to mastering this phase of the High Magic, the Chakras must be considered. You are familiar with the existence of these psychic centers of force which have been vivified in turn by "the serpent fire," as the man advances in evolution. These chakras cannot be described naturally as organs in the ordinary sense of the word, since it is not through them that the man sees or hears, as he does with his physical eyes and ears, yet it is apparently very largely upon their vivification that the power of exercising the astral senses depends, each of them, as it is developed, giving the whole astral body the power of response to a new set of vibrations.

The astral faculties may be developed in various ways, which it will be well to consider. If it were possible for a man to be isolated from all but the finest outside influences, and to unfold from the beginning in a perfect fashion, he would unquestionably develop his astral senses in regular order. In this, he would find his physical senses extending their scope until they responded to all the particular vibrations of akashic as well as of denser matter; then in orderly sequence would come sensibility to the coarser part of the astral plane, and presently the finer parts also would be included, until in due course the faculties of the highest astral perception dawned in their turn.

In real life, however, development so perfect is hardly ever known, and many a man has occasional flashes of astral perception without having the slightest appreciation of what it is. Indeed, this irregularity of development is one of the principal causes of man's common liability to error in matters of clairvoyance   a liability from which there is no escape except by careful training. Only in this latter way is there a certainty in the development of his latent powers, for, as all occultists know, it is very easy for the untrained clairvoyant to deceive himself as to the meaning and value of what he sees in astral visioning, and how easy it is to distort the astral vision completely in bringing it down into his physical consciousness.

Occasional flashes of clairvoyance sometimes come to individuals spontaneously. Such glimpses usually signify that he is approaching a stage in his evolution when these powers will naturally begin to manifest themselves, and were he to cultivate the ability he would show marked psychic talent. In other cases, the power of supernormal visioning, though still out of reach during waking life, becomes available when the body is held in the bonds of sleep. Such persons are the ones who are "warned in a dream," or dream of prophetic events which lie on ahead. Initiates often ask how the clairvoyant faculty will first be noted in themselves; how may they know when they have reached the stage when the first foreshadowings of supernormal visioning begin to manifest? Developing clairvoyant powers vary so widely in individuals that it is impossible to give a universal answer to that question; I can cover the subject for you sufficiently, however, so you can find your own answer, viz.:

Clairvoyance comes to some people in a plunge, as it were, who under the stimulus of a crisis of some kind become able to see a striking vision in a flash. Often such experience proves to be an isolated case of precognition, but it does show that the basic talent is there to be cultivated. Others begin by becoming intermittently conscious of the brilliant colors of the human aura. Often to their own surprise they see these vibrations about the heads of people with whom they come in contact. Yet others begin to find themselves, with increasing frequency, being aware of things to which those around them are blind and deaf. Others, again, seem to see faces, landscapes, or colored clouds floating before their eyes in the dark prior to going to sleep.

The clairvoyant vision of the human aura is most interesting to those who can see it, and it provides immediate insight into a person's thoughts, feelings, and character, i.e., when the aura is noted flooded with a beautiful rose color it denotes affection; a rich blue shows devotional feeling; a dull brown color indicates selfishness, and a deep scarlet anger; lurid red shows sensuality; a livid grey fear, and black hatred and malice. Little can remain hidden to the practiced eye opened to astral visioning.

In developing this power of the advanced magicians, it is well to proceed carefully, gradually, patiently, perseveringly, and persistently, beginning your first clairvoyance with the simplest experiments and exercises, and then working on to the higher and most complex stages. As the Yogis express it, "Give the right knock and in time the door will be opened unto you; but never try to break open the door, or to steal in through the window like a thief in the night." Take your time with your practice, and clairvoyance will come.

Be sure to use the crystal ball in your practice, and use it at the same time to develop your powers of concentration. In such, while using the crystal, "hold the thought for your clairvoyant development, seeing yourself "in your mind's eye" as gradually developing and unfolding the desired ESP faculties, and, at the same time, positively affirm that such is the case. Visualization and affirmation of the desired result, in your course of concentration accompanied by the use of the crystal ball, is a case of becoming what you wish to become, and is a legitimate use of the threefold magic formula of the Yogis which you have learned to use so well.

The first step in your development exercises in achieving clairvoyance or astral perception is to work with telepathy. Such exercises will tend to gradually develop and unfold the more complex and higher psychic powers. From the sensing of thoughts advance to the next stage of psychic perception which is known as Psychometry. Psychometry is really a form of clairvoyance. Its distinctive feature being that of employing a psychic "loose end" in order to establish the necessary rapport condition between the clairvoyant faculties and the senses in distant space, or past time, or both. This psychic "loose end" may be a bit of clothing, a handkerchief, a pocket knife, a piece of jewelry, a photograph, a letter, a stone, a ring, a piece of metal or mineral—anything in fact that has been associated with the person, thing, place, scene, or event with which you wish to enter into psychic *rapport* for the purpose of establishing astral visioning.

In practicing your exercises in Psychometry, you should always begin with a few moments of silence; in earnest concentration in which the crystal ball is employed as a focal point of complete attention. Then, when you feel that the desired mental condition of calmness has been acquired, you will be ready to proceed with the experiment. Have at hand the psychic "loose end" by means of which you hope to establish the rapport conditions; the psychic connection (line of communication) between your astral senses and the person, thing, place, scene or event which you wish to perceive clairvoyantly.

Now, "throw your mind blank." Then, in a few moments, you will sense that the desired psychic condition or state of mind has been reached. Then, and not until then, you should press against your forehead (or, if the object is too large, touch it with your hand) the material thing which serves as your linkage. Next, without haste let your mind drift along, making no actual effort to "see" anything in particular; just letting the "seeing" come entirely of itself. And remember this "seeing" is not as a vision within the crystal ball that will come to you, but is an image "in your mind's eye." Such is the astral sight.

Gazing into the crystal ball, let your mind proceed to drift along, in a sort of reverie without trying to "see" any particular things. Always, however, hold in the background of your mind an awareness of the material object which you are psychomotrizing. After a time, possibly not until after several successive sittings, you will begin to find that this psychic "loose end" is beginning to unwind the thread of psychic association, and you will begin to experience perception of places and scenes with which it has previously been associated.

Do not be over anxious; you cannot hurry these things, remember that over-anxiety is really an obstacle. Just let the thing work itself out. At first the perception may be dim and hazy, but do not be discouraged. Sooner or later, as you persist, the picture will become clearer and more definite, and you will perceive motion in it if there was motion in the original distant and past scene.

Sometimes you will "see" the person, thing, or event as it was in past time; again you may see it as it is at the present time, if it is still in existence. You should return to your work with the same object at different sittings; keep psychometrizing the one object until you feel sure that you have exhausted its possibilities. Then, you may take up another object, and proceed in the same way. Later on, you may go back to the first object, and you will discover how much your powers have advanced. It is largely a matter of patient, persistent practice; there is no royal road to clairvoyance—work is required.

You will find it helpful in these experiments to speak aloud, describing just what you are seeing "in your mind's eye." This will serve to enhance your vision, and make more definite the psychic pictures you perceive. For the most part, practice in private by yourself. If you work with others, be certain that they are of harmonious natures, and seek to develop their own psychic powers along with yourself. Sometimes practicing in conjunction with sympathetic persons seeking a common objective works excellently.

Do not become disturbed if you see anything startling in these psychometric experiments. You are simply the observer of events on the astral plane; and these events are merely records or reflected pictures. Consider it as though you were looking at a motion picture; it is not "real" so far as you are personally concerned. It will follow, as a matter of course, that some of the scenes which you will see in your psychometric vision will be exciting; a piece of shell from a battlefield, for instance, will connect you with some thrilling event. Be impersonal about the things you see and just observe. You will be in for some real surprises during your psychic excursions into the astral plane. For example, an old daguerreotype photograph may transport you to scenes back in the Victorian era, or an old letter will give you the "loose ends" to some strange scenes and experiences.

Do not take lightly what you see or jest about it. These are "psychic secrets" which you are bringing to light, and should be regarded as private. Occultists insist that one loses psychic gifts if he does not handle such with dignity and respect.

After you have attained a satisfactory degree of proficiency in psychometry, you will be prepared to proceed to experiments along the lines of clairvoyance without the employment of any psychic "loose ends" serving to establish the rapport with the distant of past-time scenes. Remember, however, that there is really no essential difference between such clairvoyance and that of psychometry which you have been studying.

You will probably find it easier to manifest the phenomena of present-time distant clairvoyance at first, rather than those of past-time or future-time. It is well to practice accordingly. Take it in your stride. When you have become proficient in this phase, you may then advance on to the next.

In practicing present-time distant clairvoyance, you should employ the crystal ball in the manner previously described. First, indulge in a few silent moments of concentration, using the crystal as a focal center. Then, when you feel your psychic conditions are satisfactory, proceed "throwing your mind blank" for a few moments, after which you proceed to concentrate upon the crystal for the purpose of inducing the astral vision of the happenings at some distant scene, the doings of some particular person, etc. You must "hold the thought" of that distant place or scene, or of that particular person in order to establish and set up the psychic rapport therewith.

After a little time, you will become aware that the rapport has been established. Then, allow your mind to drift along easily and without special direction, until "in your mind's eye" the astral picture begins to form. The astral picture may be nebulous at first, or else it may manifest clearly from the very start depending upon the particular psychic conditions involved in the case. Sooner or later, however, you will acquire the faculty of perceiving clear pictures. Always, there will be the impression that you are gazing into some shifting reflecting surface, something like the bosom of a tiny lake the surface of which is stirred by the passing breezes.

The astral picture so perceived "in your mind's eye" will represent the events occurring at the distant place, or the doings of the distant person, at that particular moment of time; your astral vision being much like sight through a powerful telescope. In fact, if you so desire, you may erect "The Astral Tube" to peer through in connection with such clairvoyance. Some initiates finds this helpful and holds the scene more sturdy. Such scenes viewed through "The Astral Tube" appear much as if viewed through a telescope, even the circular end of the "tube" serving to form a frame for the picture.

If you experience any difficulty in locating a distant scene or person, you will find it helpful to visualize some prominent landmark existing at that place; this will serve as a center around which the astral picture will gradually form. In case of a person whose whereabouts are unknown to you, you will find it helpful to fall back upon the psychometric method, i.e., to use a picture, letter, or other object associated with that person, in order to set up the necessary rapport condition. Having established the rapport, the object may then be discarded and the rest of the experiment conducted along the line above described. You will find "the psychometric link" very useful; employ it whenever possible.

Many initiates in clairvoyance conduct experiments in distant perception with the aid of friends. They arrange a time and date for the experiment. The distant party then carefully records just what he or she is doing at that particular time, and the clairvoyant does likewise. A comparison of these records will show conclusively just what degree of success is being obtained. Results are often remarkable, gives the clairvoyant excellent practice in the art, and develops confidence.

In practicing past-time clairvoyance, the same preliminary course is followed as in the phases of clairvoyance just described. The crystal ball, of course, is employed in concentration as always in such experimenting. The great difficulty lies in establishing a psychic rapport with the particular period in past-time in which the desired scene, event, or person existed. Using a "psychometric link" is very helpful in this regard. Once the rapport (or line of psychic communication) has been established, the "link" may be dropped. For past-time clairvoyance the reading of a story associated with that period in history aids in developing the "psychic atmosphere" of the time and scene.

Indeed, occasionally in clairvoyant experiments this principle operates without definite intent. For instance, a clairvoyant person may have been reading a story, or a page from history, in which the events of a certain time are described; and in his next session he will find himself drawn to witnessing astral events connected with that period; not the same events of which he has read, but others associated with the same general period in past-time.

Future-time clairvoyance is somewhat more complex and complicated, although the same general methods are pursued. The "connecting link" between present and future is difficult to establish in most cases. In fact, the best examples of future-time clairvoyance has been more or less spontaneous, and have taken the form of "prevision," produced involuntarily on the part of the clairvoyant. Many instances of such have been recorded in the annuals of psychical investigations. Experimental future-time clairvoyant experiences are rare.

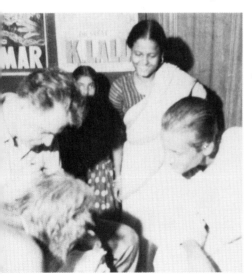

A discussion of magic.

With magicians in India. Front row: Mystic Kumar, Ormond McGill, K. Lall. Rear row: Ron Ormond and magician students.

The only general directions that can be given in such regards fall under two rules, viz.: (1) think intently of the person or place concerning whom or which you desire to know "what will be happening" at some particular time in the future; then "run your mind ahead" to that particular period of future-time. In the performance, you will finally experience that peculiar psychic "click," which I have had occasion to mention before; this will inform you that you have reached the desired point in future-time. Then let the astral picture proceed as has been described. (2) Or, while holding the person or place intently in mind, "run your mind ahead" slowly and deliberately without setting a fixed time, and, if the right conditions are present, you will see a gradually developing picture of the future events concerning that person or plac   one scene melting into another in regular sequence.

In the development of clairvoyance, astral plane phenomena, and psychic perception in all of its phases, the Yogis attach great importance to the subject of Pranayama, especially in relation to rhythmic breathing, as you have learned. They hold that the awakened and aroused Kundalini serves to vivify and energize the various chakras, connected with the Sushumna, and thus develop and unfold in themselves the powers which serve to render efficient the clairvoyant faculties and senses.

You will find that as you practice the magical arts of India that there is an interrelationship from one skill to another; as each phase developes others will in like manner be cultivated. You have been taught how to develop the powers of the Adepts and Yogis. Practice the arts. You are learning how to be a magician.

18

Yama, Yogi
Self-Development

The East Indian magicians insist that foremost in importance is the well-being and self-development of the individual practicing magic. The Yogis teach of this in their practice of Yama, which translated means "self-control." Such a definition does not begin to adequately express the full field of mental discipline and psychic power covered by the teaching and practice of Yama. To the magician, Yama is the magic which he turns inward upon himself for personal development.

The full teaching of Yama is the molding of the character of the individual by means of mental power; one practicing Yama may actually "make himself over" in character, personality, aptitudes, talents, and mental attainments. The magician especially employs Yama in the mental realm to develop the powers of mind deemed desirable, and to inhibit those which he may deem undesirable.

The basic secret for the performance of Yama is to apply "the threefold formula of the Yogi"—visualizing yourself as you wish to be or to do.

In your heart, you know full well that you are not completely all that you would like to be; you know your own shortcomings, and are aware of the qualities, characteristics, and capabilities which are lacking in your mental make-up. You know that you are "long" on certain undesirable qualities, and that you are "short" on certain desirable ones. Possibly you have thought that being as you are is the way you must remain, but the Yogis say this is not so—they affirm that you can be "as you wish to be." In the Yama teaching they point out the way by means of which you may attain this desirable objective.

Sadhu Parimal Bandhu, in his always penetrating comments on these subjects, said, "Success is due to certain qualities of mind, character, and temperament. Those who have the given qualities of the proper kind manifest the given result; those lacking in these qualities fail to manifest the result. All persons possess some of the qualities and lack others. Some are strong in certain of these qualities and weak in certain others. And every man instinctively knows in just what respect he falls short. He may not admit it to others; sometimes not even to himself; but deep down in his inner consciousness lurks the knowledge of the truth. If he could acquire the missing qualities by mere wish, he would know for just what to wish. There is no doubt about that. But he lacks the confidence and perseverence necessary for the acquirement of that which he knows he needs. Or it might be said, he is not willing to pay the price for attainment.

"Let us imagine that one of your great western scientists would announce to the world that he had discovered some remarkable chemical that would develop the shrunken and atrophied faculties of the mind, and which would render a man strong in the qualities wherein before he had been weak, what a rush there would be for the new 'miracle drug.' Millions would want it, and every man (and woman) would be able to tell for just what it was needed. He would need no diagnosis or prescription for that. Every person would know exactly his own needs, and his requirements for the drug to round out his character and command success. Unfortunately, there is no such 'miracle drug' that will produce this result; and there never will be. But the desired result can be obtained by the operation of what I call, 'the law of mental control.' "

This "law of mental control," cited by the Sadhu, is none other than the Yogi principles of self-developing—the Yama.

As I have mentioned, the practice of Yama is based on the universal Yogi threefold method of visualization, projection, and affirmation. However there is a variation from the usual form of projection.

In the performance of Yama, your first step should be to list your mental qualities, both positive and negative, and then check those which you think should be developed and strengthened, and also those which should be inhibited and restrained.

Every mental characteristic which makes up a particular individual manifests in either a positive or a negative manner. Sometimes a "positive" carried too far and unbalanced by another "positive" becomes a "negative" in effect. As for example, courage is a positive characteristic, the negative of which is cowardice. But courage, unbalanced by prudence becomes recklessness and foolhardiness, both of which are negative characteristics.

Here is the Yama rule: a "positive" characteristic is one that tends to make you stronger and more efficient; it is a success-propelling quality. A "negative" characteristic is one that tends to make you weaker and less efficient; it is a success-repelling quality. The general practice of self-development by mental power is to develop the positives, and restrain the negatives. Negatives are restrained by developing their corresponding positives. The last part of this rule is especially important; instead of trying to remove a negative quality directly, you will find it far easier to restrain it by cultivating its positive opposite. Fix this in your mind, it is an important element in the practice of Yama.

The following general list of personality characteristics will be helpful to you in charting your personal qualities for the purpose of self-development. Go carefully over this list, and check off each item according to your honest appraisal of yourself, viz.: if you are just right on a given quality, mark it with a check ($\sqrt{}$); if you are deficient in that quality, mark it with a minus sign ($-$); if you are excessive in that quality, mark it with a plus sign ($+$):

184

SELF-RESPECT	THRIFT	VANITY
PERSISTENCE	HOPE	DISCRIMINATION
INITIATIVE	CHEERFULNESS	PERCEPTION
ADAPTABILITY	KINDLINESS	MEMORY
OBSERVATION	TEMPERANCE	STABILITY
IMAGINATION	REVERENCE	TEMPER
DETERMINATION	SELF-CONTROL	AMBITION
COURAGE	PATIENCE	FAITH
TACT	EGOTISM	VERACITY
NEATNESS	JUDGMENT	JUSTICE
LOYALTY	REASONING	SERVICE
CHASTITY	ATTENTION	MORALITY
SPIRITUALITY	INDUSTRY	FRIENDLINESS
SELF-CONFIDENCE	ACQUISITIVENESS	AGGRESSIVENESS

Having conscientiously appraised yourself by marking off the foregoing list, you will know just which of your qualities require strengthening, just which require toning-down, and just which need repressing (or controlling). In the work of strengthening, you proceed directly by applying "The Threefold Method of the Yogi" to the task. In the work of toning-down, and of repressing, however, you proceed indirectly, i.e., by applying "The Threefold Method of the Yogi" to the task of developing more strongly the opposite quality associated with the particular quality requiring controlling.

"The Threefold Method of the Yogi" of visualization, projection, and affirmation is applied in Yama along the general lines as you have learned. Here are specific instructions:

VISUALIZATION IN YAMA

Make a practice of thinking and picturing yourself as being that which you want to be in relation to the personal characteristic you are developing in yourself. This may be done in two basic ways: (1) in formal sessions of concentrate visualization employing the crystal ball as your focus of concentration; and (2) by holding informal thoughts and visualizations within yourself whenever possible during the day and night by means of holding in "the mind's eye" the mental-picture from time to time. The first constitutes the way of the regular psychic self-development treatment; the second constitutes the associated treatment.

In both of these "self-development treatments" you will find it helpful in holding the definite ideal and mental-picture, if you will fix in your mind the characteristic physical actions and general behavior of a person manifesting the desire quality, and then picture yourself as acting out the part in general physical demeanor. There is a close correlation between physical actions and mental states. Each act and react upon the other, and are really the two poles of the same thing. Accordingly, always mentally-picture yourself as "acting out" the physical part expressing the mental attitude you are seeking to develop by Yama visualization. The better you "play the part" in such visualization, the better will be the result.

Several well-known psychologists speak of this matter:

Professor R. P. Halleck says, "By inducing an expression we can often cause its allied emotion. Actors have frequently testified to the fact that emotion will arise if they go through the appropriate muscular movements. In talking to a character on the stage, if they clench the fist and frown, they often find themselves becoming really angry; if they start with counterfeit laughter, they find themselves growing cheerful."

Professor William James says , "Whistling to keep up courage is no mere figure of speech. On the other hand, sit all day in a moping posture, sigh, and reply to everything with a dismal voice, and your melancholy lingers. If we wish to conquer undesirable tenencies in ourselves, we must assiduously, and in the first instance coldbloodedly, go through the outward movements of those contrary dispositions, which we wish to cultivate. Smooth the brow, brighten the eye, contract the dorsal back rather than the ventral front aspect of the frame, and speak in a major key, pass the genial compliment, and your heart must indeed be frigid if it does not gradually thaw.

William James further says, "Can one fancy the state of rage and picture no ebullition in the chest, no flushing of the face, no dilation of the nostrils, no clenching of the teeth, no impulse to vigorous action, but in their stead limp muscles, calm breathing, and a placid face." The Yogis even go so far as to claim that if one deliberately counterfeits the rate and rhythm of breathing manifested in any particular emotion state, or mental state, he will find that emotional or mental state becoming reproduced and represented in his own thoughts and feelings."

Professor Maudsley says, "The specific muscular action is not merely an exponent of passion, but truly an essential part of it. If, while the features are fixed in the expression of one passion, we try to call up in the mind a different passion, we shall find it impossible to do so."

These authorities have shown sound psychology behind "acting a part" in your visualizing. In other words, not merely visualizing yourself as having the desired quality or qualities, but, also, as manifesting them in action. See yourself as acting out the part, as going through the motions, as expressing in outward form the desired personal quality. Visualize first one desired characteristic, and then another, and so on, until you have acted out in mental vision the whole list of desired characteristics.

Furthermore, whenever you think of yourself in connection with anything associated with or related to the characteristic in question, be sure to think of and visualize yourself as possessed of and manifesting that characteristic. Get into the way of thinking and seeing yourself manifesting in outer form that inner state. In this way, you will establish a psychic path over which your will can freely travel when it goes outward into action; you are establishing the new trait as part of your being.

Equally true, you should never allow yourself to think of, or to picture yourself, as manifesting the undesirable characteristic which you are seeking to repress. This, because such acts of attention tends to strengthen these undesirable characteristics; you must not "feed" them by attention, instead you must "starve" them by inattention. And, while thus "starving" an undesirable negative quality, you must be at work "feeding" the desirable positive characteristic which you wish to establish in your being.

In a nutshell, forget the negatives and develop the positives.

PROJECTION IN YAMA

In the performance of Yama, or self-development by the Yoga method, you should apply the element of projection, as you have learned it, with precision, vigor, and determinination. However Yama calls for a slight variation in the method employed.

In projection for psychic work and magic, the visualization is usually projected outward to the akasha, or to the chitta of other persons. In Yama, however, the effect is desired to be produced upon yourself. Consequently, there must be an inward projection, and the Yogis state that the projection must be to both body and mind, in this regard.

The visualization once obtained in the proper form and degree, and the affirmations made in the same way (as you will be instructed below), the ideal-picture or thought-form should be projected by two acts. First an act of will, *spreading it out* so that it will permeate the entire brain; and also sending it *down* so that it will permeate every muscle in the body. This is important, as there is a close relationship between physical actions and mental states in self-development. In this way, both brain and muscles are influenced and

The gala festival of Dasehra, celebrating the magical conquest of evil by good. On the last day the people burn the giant effigies of evil gods.

animated with the vibratory force of the mental-picture, and are set to reproduce the visualized mental state and physical action.

This act of Yama Projection is readily acquired; simply spread out and project into yourself the vibratory forces of the visualized-picture by an action of will. The knack will come with a little practice.

Also it is well, from time to time, to supplement the work of this projection by an occasional deliberate "acting out" of the physical actions of the desired mental or emotional characteristic. Practice this in private; practice before your mirror, as if you were rehearsing a part in a play. For that matter, you are really "rehearsing" in such case, but not for a play; rather for real life and action.

In such rehearsal or acting-out of the projected ideal and picture, you are not only making it easier for the will to manifest in similar physical actions, and consequent mental states; you are also, at the same time and in the same way, giving an "astral" (akashic etheric form) to the mental and emotional forces which have *projected* into the brain and body. The more thoroughly you rehearse and practice this "acting out" process, the more powerful does that subtle form become in fact.

AFFIRMATION IN YAMA

Affirmation is called mantrayama by the Yogis; apply it as you have previously been instructed in connection with the practice of Yama or self-development. The general principle consists in expressing in verbal form, either mentally or vocally, the idea or thought, the picture or concept, which you have already visualized and are about to project. This serves to crystallize the thought, and gives it body and form; also, according to Yoga teaching, there are certain effects produced by the vibratory influence of thought-filled words.

What you have learned of the power of affirmations applies equally in the particular form of "treatment" known as Yama. In addition, there are two special points concerning this application of affirmation to this process, viz., (1) the choice of suggestive words, and (2) the "second person" method of directing the affirmation.

Considering the choice of suggestive words, you should first acquaint yourself with the various terms defining or being analogous to the particular quality you wish to cultivate and develop. Next select the most inspiring and animating words from the list—the words or terms being selected should have the greatest suggestive power, and the greatest vibratory power. These words should be capable of arousing the highest degree of incentive feeling in yourself.

For instance, let us suppose that you wish to cultivate the quality of courage within yourself, if such happened to be a quality in which you are lacking. By refering to the dictionary, you will find the following synonyms of courage: heroism, bravery, intrepidity, valor, valiantness, gallantry, daring, firmness, hardihood, boldness, dauntlessness, resolution, etc. A further search of the dictionary will give you more synonyms of each of these terms. Make a list of them, and then repeat them to yourself, letting each work sink into your mind, awakening in your mind their respective vibration or responses.

188

Say them as a mantram; you will find that some of these words will fairly set your soul on fire, and will awaken suggestive vibrations of desire, ambition, seeking, striving, etc., accompanied by a corresponding impulse to action. Write down the special words that strike the most responsive chord in your being; letting the others rest until you place them in a secondary list. In this way you will have developed an inspiring list of suggestive words for yourself to employ as your affirmation; in this case for the cultivation of courage.

The same thing you will find true of any other terms denoting a desired quality or characteristic. For instance, suppose you wish to affirm the quality of stability. Here you will run across the associated terms of tenacity, fixedness, purpose, doggedness, determination, firmness, resolution, unwavering, persistent, persevering, steadiness, abiding, strong, durable, steadfastness, enduring, etc. Some of these words you will find strongly hit home to you. When you find them, make a list of them, and thereafter affirm and assert them to and of yourself. You will find that such special words will fill you with the desired vibrations, and will arouse in yourself the firm and fierce determination to express them in your character.

Also, energizing suggestive words will give a clearer outline to your visualization, for you will mentally picture yourself as manifesting the particular physical action and mental states which are triggered by these special words. Moreover, they will serve to give additional force to your projection; visualization, projection, and affirmation really being but parts of the same fundamental activity of thought and will in this process; in direct ratio each enforcing the other and blending into a powerful manifestation.

Let us now consider point two of Affirmation in Yama, which is directing the affirmation in "the second person." Western teachers of affirmation will tell you to affirm in the first person, as, "I am courageous;" "I am stable and persistent;" etc. This is based on sound psychology, but the Yogis instruct that in using Yama, the initiate is advised to make the affirmation in the form of a command or statement to himself. In other words, give yourself the command in the second person. For example, John Doe (or whatever your name may be) you are courageous, you are filled with courage, you are brave, daring, intrepid, bold, etc." Or, "John Doe, you are tenacious, fixed of purpose, dogged, determined, resolute, steady, persistent, persevering, steadfast, enduring; you are filled with stick-to-itiveness; you never give up; you have fixed purposes, and pursue them to the determined end, etc."

In other words, you should conduct this work of affirmation just as were you giving a "treatment" to another person, and seeking to cultivate in him the particular characteristic which you are seeking to cultivate in yourself. The Yogis say that one talks best and gives instructions to his innerself that way.

You must of course back up this practice of Yama by actual manifestation of the desired quality or characteristic in performance in your daily life. Let your thought take form in action, as often as possible. Play as often as possible in real life that which you have been rehearsing and "playing out" mentally in your exercises.

You now have the technique for the practice of Yama. Use it. You can make yourself anew!

THE SECRET FORMULA OF THE MAGICIANS

Sadhu Parimal Bandu spoke confidentially, "I will tell you one of the deep secrets of the magicians. I shall only give you the gist, but enough so the clever can use the formula: Adepthood comes from turning Yama within upon the magic powers. The result is a chain-reaction, the Yama developing the Powers and the Powers developing the Yama. It is true magic."

I made my notes. The Sadhu leaned forward and whispered, "And the heart of the secret is to turn Yama upon the Serpent."

19
The Great "I Am"

"I AM" is the center of your being. In the chapter "Conclusions of the Journey" in the book, *Religious Mysteries of the Orient,* it was written, as spoken by the Sages, that in all the Universe there is but one of yourself. You are absolutely unique and individual. You are "I AM." As a living soul incarnate, you are in a state of constant evolution and will take part in many experiences in which are involved factors of being master, or mastered, or both. Influences are constantly seeking to affect one. When Sadhu Parimal Bandhu first spoke to me regarding acquiring the ability to nullify the influence of magic by others from outside sources, I was inclined to minimize it. He repeatedly assured me that such knowledge must be included in a text dealing with the real magic of India, as this aspect is very much practiced by the magicians.

I am certain that during this study, the thought must have occurred to you that unless there exists some means of self-protection from the various forms of psychic influence, every person is more or less subject to such magic. You must have asked the question, "If I can learn to exert such influence, what is there to protect me from such influence from others, should there be a need?"

The question is an important one, and the magicians have an answer to it, as I will explain in this concluding chapter of this book.

There is a fundamental law of nature which may be expressed as follows: for every bane, nature supplies an antidote. The Hindus express it in their aphorism, "Wherever there is a disease, there exists a cure for it." The truth is applicable not only to the physical world, but also to the mental—and to that phase of the mental which we call the psychical.

In the first place, on the psychic plane there exists a corresponding analogy to what on the physical plane is referred to as immunization. All people throughout the world have acquired various types of immunizations. Certain diseases once very destructive in their effects have now almost died out from people in certain countries. Yet, when the people from an immune country visit another, frequently the natives thereof will contract the diseases in question. In the same way, it is known that certain unsanitary conditions in a tropical area will produce sickness and often death to Europeans, whereas the natives of those regions are unaffected. Thus, you see, there are many illustrations of this universal law of immunization in Nature, which is exerted whenever there is need for it. As I have stated, we find this law manifest on the psychic plane as well.

Up to a certain point, most persons are immune to psychic influence of lower magnitude. Their subconscious mental forces erect a barrier against such influences of a low degree of intensity. As the greater part of psychic influence is below that degree, they are largely free from same. When the psychic influence rises above low intensity, then this immunity is overcome and the majority of persons are more or less subject to such influences, as for most people no immunity of high psychic influence has ever been developed.

The higher degree of psychic influence, as a general rule, is manifested only by those persons who have mastered the arts of magic. There are, however, certain exceptional individuals of the race who seem to have awakened a knowledge of the use of such powers almost instinctively. Inasmuch as the immunization to psychic influence is very low in Nature, it behoves the individual to learn how to master such mental-magic by magic of his own.

Sadhu Parimal Bandhu said on this point, "I would caution all persons to refrain from feeling akin to fear in relation to magical influence from outside sources. Fear, in itself, is one of the most negative and weakening mental states known to man. Fear renders negative the most positive individual, if freely indulged in. I ask you to remember that no matter how potent may be the mendacious currents, there are none that may not be rendered impotent and ineffectual by one's own mind and will. Each and every individual has within himself and under his control a force that will render him immune to all undesirable influence. Such is the law of Nature; it makes no bane without its antidote; it supplies the means of self-protection to everyone, and always furnishes a defensive weapon to match every offensive one."

The Yoga teaching is that the individual may render himself immune from all detrimental psychic influence (or influence that is not desired) by means of a cultivated mental attitude established as a subconscious habit for resisting and repelling these influence. The magician having established this "habit," need give little more attention to the matter.

Moreover, one may erect about himself "a protective aura," which will serve as a barrier to the entrance of thought currents of unwanted psychic influence. Again, one may create a state of Dynamic Egohood (I AM) of such psychic intensity that no undesirable thought-influence can prevail against its defensive power. Esoteric teaching contains many important items along this line which I shall call to your attention. Also the same principles which will be given you for the purpose of psychic self-protection, will also tend to create and develop in you a high degree of psychic positivity which will render far more powerful your own manifestations of psychic influence (magic).

All occultists are familiar with the oriental wisdom which asserts that in each individual is a center of psychic invulnerability known as "the I AM Consciousness," or as the Yogis call it "the Ahamkara Assertion." Oriental teachings are filled with reference to it, and with instructions concerning its development.

192

This high state of Ahamkara Consciousness may be described simply as the awareness that you, the individual, are a center of consciousness, being, and power in the Great Universal Consciousness, which has infinite power. In other words, you are a focalized center of universal creative energy (combined mind and prana) established by the cosmic laws in the universal substance of Akasha. The Yogis affirm that the mere knowing of this cosmic kinship brings a tremendous increase in power to the individual; while a still further unfoldment of that "knowing" makes of the man a superman.

Ego Consciousness is more than an awareness of the outside world, or of one's own body as distinct from the bodies of others. It is more than even the awareness of one's own mind as unique. It is difficult to describe this plane of consciousness to those who have not attained it, but it may be stated as an awareness of individuality, rather than an awareness of personality. Many persons never have more than a misty idea of such a mental attitude; they take themselves for granted, and never turn the gaze inward.

Sadhu Parimal Bandhu explains it well: "We are conscious of our own existence. We know, first of all, our physical bodies. Then, we know our sensations, our emotion, our desires, our ideas, our thoughts, and our acts. Lastly, each of us knows a certain 'Something Within' which is more fundamental than all these instruments and tools, physical and mental. This each of us calls 'I' and states its existence as 'I AM!' This 'I' is at the center of the normal consciousness of each individual. Yet it is not a part of his sensations or emotions, his feelings or thoughts. What is it? Ask your own consciousness, and it answers merely 'I AM I' the Self of Myself. We cannot describe it. We cannot classify it with anything else. We cannot separate ourselves from it. We cannot stand off and examine it. It underlies all else in our consciousness.

"Each of us bases his Selfhood on this inner consciousness. We say, 'I am conscious that I AM! Therefore, I know that I exist! The ego, or 'I,' will always be found at the center of consciousness; and it will always affirm positively and without reservation the positive truth and fact of its absolute existence, in the invariable and inevitable statement, 'I AM!' This 'I AM' is a center—a focalized, concentrated center—of the illumined spirit within the individual; when it probes the depths of its own being, and explores its own 'deep of deeps' it must ever report, in the words of the ancient Hindu Vedas, 'TAT TVAM ASI,' or 'That Art Thou!' or, in the words of age-old Oriental Scripture, 'I Am THAT I Am!'—all hold the same meaning."

This then, is the oriental wisdom concerning the "seat of power in the individual"—the throne which he "the king of self," issues his commands and announces his will. The teaching is that "the seat of power," when consciously occupied and maintained, is impregnable to all outside assaults, no matter how powerful these may be. This is the seat of self-mastery—the Castle of self-protection!

Once recognized and established, this Ego-Consciousness never leaves one. The famous author Paul Brunton refers to it as "The Overself," in which one may take refuge, and from which tower of strength he may defy adversity. From it he may direct conditions, master circumstances, and dominate events. It is the center of his being; the "solid rock" from which the magician hurls his

Goodbyes to many Hindu friends who helped us learn of the mysticism and magic of India.

magic, and from which he cannot be dislodged. From it you can exercise freely and assert fearlessly your poise and power, your dominion and strength. It is of the utmost importance that you seek and find this great center of power within yourself.

DEVELOPING AND UNFOLDING THE DYNAMIC EGO-CONSCIOUSNESS

The following are the instructions given by the magicians for arousing and unfolding within yourself the Dynamic Ego-Consciousness, which is THE GREAT "I AM!" You must learn to recognize, realize, and manifest the 'I' in yourself. The discovery and development of this Dynamic Ego-Consciousness; this conscious of your real self; this "I Am I" will lead to the discovery of a new world of power for you, the individual. It forms a most important phase in the entire structure of oriental wisdom. Master this development:

Employing the crystal ball, as you have learned to use it, proceed to concentrate for the Dynamic Ego-Consciousness. After a period of brief contemplation, in which you "throw the mind blank," you concentrate your attention and thought upon the idea that you are the master self or your selfhood—the center of power in your realm. Then visualize yourself symbolically as existing as an actual entity at the center of your mental realm. See and feel yourself as using all your mental faculties and powers—all these being the instruments with which you express the power and reality which is you! While holding this thought, make the following Mantram (affirmation) of egohood:

"I AM! I Am I! I am the center of power in my being. My body is an instrument of my expression and manifestation. Body and mind are mine to use; they belong to me, but they are not me. I AM over and above them. I am their master and they will do my bidding, for I Am asserting my dominion over them, for I Am the king on the throne of my mental and physical kingdom. All these subordinate elements are for my use, and they will obey my commands when I direct them with the full consciousness of my I AM. I Am I. I Am the Master Self. I Am the Overself!"

This mantram of affirmation, accompanied by the appropriate meditation of concentrated visualization, will arouse and awaken in you the sense of your existence as the Master Self—the unique and individual entity which is YOU which inhabits "your" body and uses "your" mind to express itself. Practice this method until you feel that you have reached the full consciousness of your Reality, your Power, and Dominion. You will never be in doubt when this stage is reached; the message from within will be unmistakable. You will experience confidence and power such as you have never had when you reach this realization of Egohood.

After you have perfected yourself in the conscious realization of inner power and dominion as the Overself, proceed to practice the following advanced method, viz,:

195

Use concentrated visualization, as previously instructed, directing your thought, attention, and visualization faculties to the creation of a mental-picture of idealization: see your Master Self, your Ego, your "I," the I AM as the center of your world of experience; all the rest of the world revolving around you, in a great circling swing, like a great wheel revolving around its hub.

As directions, this reads like a formula for arrogance and conceit, but the I AM as used by the magicians is something very different from personal egotism, for it is not your physical (personal) self which you are making the center of your reality, it is your master self, your real inner self (entirely independent of physical body and mind) which you are expressing in I AM. You are in truth such a center in creation . . . for remember, in all Creation there is but the one of you; you are absolutely unique and individual.

You must have this consciousness of your inner reality to be a magician.

The Oriental Sages state, "The Universe is infinite; it has its center everywhere, and its circumference nowhere; in its every point it may assert that position to be the center of all the rest."

See and feel yourself as that center; to bring it home to yourself in visualization, see yourself to be the Sun, and all the rest as planets revolving around yourself. And accompany this visualization with the following affirmation:

"I AM! I Am I! I AM A DYNAMIC CENTER OF POWER IN THE UNIVERSE. I Am a psychic center radiating in every direction to all the rest of the world. I Am the center of universal dynamic power. I work effects upon the plastic substance of the material world. I Am truly a master of magic. My visualizations become material realities. My mental-patterns gather around them material form and response. My ideals become real. I Am truly a master of magic. I Am a creative center of expression and manifestation. By my thought I express my creative energy in material form; I radiate my power. I attract to myself, by the great 'Law of Mental Attraction,' all that I need in order to express myself in my mental creations. And, by the same Law, I repel from myself all that is opposed to the realization of my ideals. I am the master of circumstances, and create conditions and environment. I do all of this by the Universal Dynamic Magical-Psychic Power of which I AM a center of force, strength, and activity."

This affirmation will establish you as a source of power. You will always be able to hold firmly your positive mental attitude and the power associated therewith, by the exercise of such visualization and affirmation, accompanied by the associated projection within yourself, all having as their ideal the assertion of the power of Egohood possessed by you as a unique individual in the Universe in recognition of your I AM stature.

Likewise, possessed by you is your absolute immunity from all psychic assaults. In this regard, "hold the thought" and mental-picture of yourself as the master self—the dynamic "I." At the same time, confidentally make the following affirmation: "I AM! I Am I! I am a center of dynamic power. I am safe. I am secure. Nothing can harm me. I am a Master of conditions and circumstances. I am a center of Universal Power, and the All-Power is back of

196

me and supporting me. I am the master of magic, and I assert my power over all circumstances. I Am I. I AM!"

The Yogis have condensed this affirmation in a one sentence rhythmic mantram as, "I AM I, I, I, I, MYSELF, I AM!" They semi-sing it along in a cadence of rhythm. Made postively and with inner understanding it will raise you to the position of poise and power; of mastery and dominion.

You now have the Yoga method of Akamkara ("The Assertion of the Ego") as taught in the ancient Sankhya philosophies of India. Rightly understood and applied it becomes a wonderful instrument of power and protection to the individual. Its mantrams all center around asserting the Real Self as "I AM" or "I AM I" or a rhythmic "I, I, I, I, I, I, I." Its tremendous vibrations, according to the oriental teachers, produce most miraculous results. This secret of the Mantram of Ahamkara is one of the great secrets of the Master Magicians.

There is a special mantram in Yoga which is designed for psychic self-protection. Remember, as always in using mantrams you must "hold the thought," for it is the inner mantram which is the most important; hold the thought of the truth of the statement and its inner meaning. Here is the Yoga mantram designed for individual protection, viz.:

"I assert and affirm my Individuality as a center of force, power, and will. I deny to anyone the power to affect me adversely, or contrary to my best interests. Nothing can adversely affect me. My mind and thoughts are my own, and I refuse admittance to them of all unwelcomed thought-influences. My desires are my own, and I refuse to have them influenced by outside psychic forces. My will is my own, and I charge it with full power to repel, throw off, and reject all undesirable influences from outside sources. I Am surrouned by an atmosphere of positive will and dynamic psychic power, which protects me absolutely. My inner power scatters into bits all thought-influences directed against me, no matter from what source they may proceed. I am the Master of my Being—I Am the Master Self. I rest secure on the foundation of my awakened Egohood and Individuality. I assert my 'I AM' against all attempts to influence or move me against my will. I am dynamic! I am a positive center of living will!"

In the performance of this mantram/affirmation, you will note how it has raised your mental vibrations to such an extent that you can actually feel that you are absolutely immune and protected from adverse psychic influences. The Yogis also teach "The Protective Aura" for this purpose, in which an occasional flash of visualization, projection, and affirmation they create a psychic atmosphere or protection about themselves. They refer to it as "a psychic barrier" which will defy, repel, and cast off any adverse thought-influences. The visualization is pictured in the mind as a protective aura surrounding one's self.

Occultists call the protective aura "The Ring Pass Not," and employ it to surround themselves with a "psychic ring" of projective Akashic Substance built up and maintained by the will and strongly charged with prana. It is said not only to repel unwanted influences, but to "shock" invaders.

The Yogis state that they charge the protective aura with a strong flow of prana by rhythmic breathing, and then project the current of prana to the protective aura by the combined effort of thought, will, and affirmation.

Swami Ramavedananda says on the subject, "From the castle wall which you have built around you, will rebound the arrow and spears which have been hurled against it. They will rebound and fly back to those who sent them, often taking lodgment in the bosom of the senders if they have been sent with the intent of wounding you. Or, like a great mirror, it will throw back into the eyes of the senders, blinding and dazzling them, the rays of psychic vibrations which they have directed for the purpose of harmful influence. But, know you, O Chela, that you yourself will not be the sender-back of these adverse forces. Be never as a black magician, and, lo, beware for the thrusting of evil, acting to and the reaction backward resulting from it, will attach to the Karma of the sender and attacker. The Great Law thus works, and attaches the results of actions where they rightfully belong."

The Yoga teachings hold that nature gives greater power to protective thought than to attacking thought. Only ignorance can make a person susceptible to adverse psychic influence. Knowledge is Protective Power in the realm of the psychic, and the mere positive affirmation, "I deny all power of influencing me adversely, to any and all minds and wills, or any and every person," when made from the position of Ahamkara, will be sufficient to defeat and deflect all adverse psychic influence.

Parimal Bandu added, "When you experience a sudden and unaccountable impulse to do a certain thing which you believe adverse to your welfare, affirm: 'You do not belong to me or mine; go back to those who sent you; go back where you belong!' "

In concluding this book on the real magic of India, I will emphasize that in The Great "I AM" you have one of the profoundest secrets of oriental wisdom which is connected not only to the phase of psychic self-protection, but also with the manifestation of each and every form of magic which has been considered. It has deep significance, for in the Egohood you are not only made strong in protective-power, but also strong in expressive power.

The position of the magician taken under the Mantram of Ahamkara is the "post-powerful" known to occult teaching. It is the position of the master. From it you may manifest any of the mental and psychic powers with a wonderfully intensified effect. In the ancient writings of India related to magic, this mental position is referred to as "The Place of Power," for remember it is your real self, your inner self, your soul!

The venerable Hindu epic, "Mahabharata" tells its countless millions of readers down through the ages, that:

"There is an Everlasting Soul—the Eternal, Unimaginable Soul!
The weapon cannot pierce it through, nor waste it the consuming fire;
The liquid water melt it not, nor dries it up the parching wind.
Impenetrable and unburned; impermeable and undried;
Perpetual, even wandering, firm, indissoluble, permanent,
Invisible unspeakable dwells it forever the Real Self of Self!"

198

As I completed the writing of my notes for the preparation of this text in Calcutta, the Sadhu spoke to me, "I have given you the secrets of the practice of oriental magic as it is taught by the Masters. This is 'the hidden knowledge.' Now, indeed, does East meet West. Some will use this knowledge and achieve mastery while other will fail, depending upon the talents of the individual. Thus is as it has ever been in the Orient, and thus it will likewise be in the Occident. I can, however, give you the invaluable schedule of development as used by the successful magicians. The schedule is seven in number each phase of which should be mastered in ascending order before proceeding on to the next. This is of such importance that I box it specially."

1. Study and learn well the principles of Yoga as used in magic.
2. Master Pranayama
   a. Learn how to effectively use rhythmic breathing.
   b. Increase your pranic energy, and learn how to tap the infinite supply.
   c. Use your psychic nervous system. Awaken the kundalini, and cause it to mount the sushumna channel and activate the seven major chakras, aiming your goal at the ultimate "flowering of the thousand petalled lotus." Such is the heart of magical power. Such will bring illumination to your entire being.
3. In the light of your illumination, now develop your powers of concentration, mind control, and use of Creative Mind Principles.
4. In the light of your illumination, now develop your powers of visualization, projection, and affirmation, using the methods in which you have been instructed.
5. Turn your awakened powers inward upon yourself in the practice of Yama. Develop your being toward superiority in everyway, and, remember, turn Yama upon the development of the kundalini powers.
6. Having cultivated, thus, your basic powers learn how to apply them in the performance of the various forms of magic and mysticism in actual demonstration. Practice maya, psychic influencing, mental broadcasting, the control of circumstances and events, etc., and finally work towards the high magic of Creative Mind with its accompanying powers of Astral Plane (ESP) phenomena.
7. Recognize your individuality, and the mastery and invunerability of your selfhood.

"This schedule of development, as used by the successful magicians, brings each phase of development interrelated upon each phase and squares the ratio of your progress in the mastery of the finer forces of Nature. It is the method of training employed by the most elect. It will make magic in time become as a way of life unto you, and as such becomes 'second nature' to your being will you then truly be a magician.

"The truths I have given you and the knowledge therefrom will ever stand eternal. One last word I would admonish: use these powers wisely and in worthy purpose. Do not prostitute the magical powers for selfish uses, and remember there is 'a boomerang law' to the practice of magic, as evil attracts evil, so if employed as black arts the effects of evil come unto the magician. Conversely good attracts good; be a white magician and in like manner all good will befall you. Such is the law of magic."

Sadhu Parimal Bandu left for the Himalayas. Ron Ormond and I returned to America. With me was this manuscript which made possible bringing you *The Mysticism and Magic of India*.

Index

201

203